What People

Industrial Real Estate Investing and Management

My development company has constructed hundreds of industrial buildings, many of which I own as personal investment properties. I have known Obie since 1996 and can say without reservation that he is the consummate industrial real estate professional and his new book is right on the money.
Don Pickett, Don Pickett & Associates

This book does an excellent job of laying out the steps necessary to buy, manage, and sell industrial buildings, and it would certainly expedite the learning curve for new commercial real estate agents.
Michael R. Porte, SIOR, Sr Vice President, Newmark Pearson Commercial Realty

This book is ideal as a supplemental text for college courses in commercial real estate and MBA curricula.
Cuthbert L. Scott III, PhD, Associate Professor Emeritus, School of Business and Economics, Indiana University Northwest

Good advice in simple terms. Business owners who wish to purchase their own industrial buildings should definitely read this book.
Ray Kulina (retired), Western Region Sr Credit Manager, U.S. Small Business Administration

It is undeniably apparent that you are an expert on this topic and your credentials make you the ideal person to write this book. The writing is engaging and the outline is spot on.

Michele Matrisciani, *New York Times* bestselling editor and Sr Editor, McGraw Hill Publishing

Industrial Real Estate Investing and Management

A Comprehensive Guide to Buying, Leasing, and Selling Industrial Buildings

Previous Books

The Guide to Successful Living
ISBN 0-9629226-0-9

007Obie
ISBN 978-0-692-78297-2

Industrial Real Estate Investing and Management

A Comprehensive Guide to Buying,
Leasing, and Selling Industrial Buildings

Obie R. Silverwood

BUSINESS
BOOKS

London, UK
Washington, DC, USA

CollectiveInk

First published by Business Books, 2024
Business Books is an imprint of Collective Ink Ltd.,
Unit 11, Shepperton House, 89 Shepperton Road, London, N1 3DF
office@collectiveinkbooks.com
www.collectiveinkbooks.com
www.collectiveinkbooks.com/business-books

For distributor details and how to order please visit the 'Ordering' section on our website.

Text copyright: Obie R. Silverwood 2023

ISBN: 978 1 80341 604 5
978 1 80341 640 3 (ebook)
Library of Congress Control Number: 2023943889

A CIP catalogue record for this book is available from the British Library.

Design: Lapiz Digital Services

UK: Printed and bound by CPI Group (UK) Ltd, Croydon, CR0 4YY
Printed in North America by CPI GPS partners

We operate a distinctive and ethical publishing philosophy in
all areas of our business, from our global network of authors to
production and worldwide distribution.

Note from the author about the use of pronouns
Use of the masculine pronouns *he, him,* and *his* predominates
in this book. The choice of masculine language when referring
to professionals such as real estate brokers and appraisers is
simply to prevent the repetition of awkward constructions
such as "he or she," or "him- or herself." It is not to be
interpreted as gender stereotyping in the subject area under
discussion.

Contents

Introduction

Along the Pacific Coast Highway near Malibu there was a little real estate office with a big sign that read, "ONE GOOD REAL ESTATE INVESTMENT CAN BE WORTH A LIFETIME OF LABOR." As a teenage surfer, I read that sign many times on my way to the beach. Years later, in my early commercial real estate brokerage career, I was canvassing for listings and asked the owner of an industrial building if he wanted to sell it. He was an older fellow and responded, "No, the rent from that building is my retirement income." His answer and that Malibu real estate sign planted seeds in my thinking that enabled me to retire relatively young, because I invested in industrial buildings.

Industrial buildings are a source of long-term, secure rental income and a means of protecting invested capital from inflation erosion. They are tangible assets that allow "hands on" control, as compared to stocks and bonds, which are digital assets with many layers of intermediaries affecting their value, over which investors have little or no control. And, for investors who purchase an industrial property as an operating facility for their business, there is the additional benefit of building equity rather than just paying rent.

To be fair, in comparison, income properties do have the disadvantage of property tax, insurance, and maintenance expenses during vacancy periods. On the other hand, their values tend to be more stable than stocks and bonds, which can drop 30% overnight, or go to zero.

This book shares my 47 years of experience as an industrial real estate broker and investor. It details the steps I take to purchase, exchange, construct, manage, and sell industrial buildings. It is a comprehensive guide for investors; a valuable reference tool for commercial real estate brokers, agents, attorneys, appraisers, property managers, and business owners; and an ideal study text for university real estate degree and Master of Business Administration (MBA) curricula.

My credentials: On graduating from business school, I was employed for five years by the National Cash Register Company, marketing commercial computer systems for accounting application, which rendered me expert accounting skills. My commercial real estate brokerage career began in 1976 at the Newport Beach office of Grubb & Ellis. In 1981 I opened my own brokerage in Irvine, California, specializing in industrial properties. I have personally transacted millions of square feet of industrial building sales, exchanges, and leases, representing clients and for my own portfolio. Investing in industrial real estate provided me with a multimillion-dollar net worth and adequate income to retire from brokerage in my mid-forties. I hold a Bachelor of Science (BSc) degree in Business Administration, specialized in Marketing, from California State University at Long Beach (1970), with graduate studies at Whittier Law School (2001), and I have been continuously licensed in good standing as a California Department of Real Estate broker since 1977, and have completed all required Continued Professional Education courses during that period.

1. Why Invest in Industrial Buildings?

Compared to other real estate investments, and in addition to the income they generate, I prefer industrial buildings for the following reasons:

A. Small, free-standing industrial buildings are relatively affordable and a good exchange vehicle to move up from owning residential rental properties.

B. Industrial building leases are typically three to five years, or longer, which minimizes tenant turnover and vacancy marketing hassles.

C. Most industrial building leases require the tenant to maintain the property in virtually all respects, which minimizes management work and expenses.

D. Industrial buildings are utilitarian in design. Most are concrete tilt-up or Butler-style metal construction with 10% to 20% of their square footage built out as offices in the front and with truck doors on the sides. The buildings are situated on land parcels large enough to accommodate property line setbacks, paved parking and yard areas, and landscaping. This basic layout is acceptable to most tenants, which minimizes the costs of transitioning from one tenant to the next, and makes them easier to market.

Comparatively, rental houses and apartment building leases are for one year or less, posing tenant turnover work and expense. Also, most residential rentals require the property owner to service the heating, ventilation, and air conditioning (HVAC), water heater, plumbing, and other mechanical problems; and, if it is a multitenant residential building, the property owner must maintain the common areas, such as laundry rooms, landscaping, and parking lots, and pay for common-use utilities.

Likewise, most office building and retail properties have common areas the owner must maintain while also providing utilities, cleaning, and trash disposal. On filling vacancies, new office and retail tenants seldom want the same floor space layout as the previous tenant, resulting in costly and time-consuming renovations. Consequently, residential, office, and retail properties usually necessitate the expense of employing a leasing agent and property manager.

Unlike industrial properties, which are available in small, free-standing sizes, most office and retail buildings are larger properties that require substantial capital to buy. Consequently, they are not as affordable for first-time investors, and do not make convenient vehicles for exchanging up from residential rentals.

2. Buying a Building

The following pages will lead you through the steps I take to buy industrial properties, which include:

A. Finding a property to buy.

B. Evaluating a prospective property's economic feasibility.

C. Evaluating a property's physical characteristics.

D. Making an offer to purchase and negotiating.

E. Entering into a purchase agreement.

F. Opening, processing, and closing escrow.

It is advisable to employ an experienced commercial real estate broker (see **Subject 51: D (1) Finding a good commercial real estate broker**) to represent you in your first purchase of industrial real estate. Whether you do so or not, this book will guide you with the assumption that you are going to perform all of the property acquisition and management functions yourself, because knowing how to do so will enable you to better judge the performance of your broker and optimize your industrial property ownership experience.

My Number One Rule in buying a property is, **"Avoid partners."** Generally, they are nothing but trouble and a very good way to ruin friendships or family relations. If you think you need a partner because you don't have enough cash to make the purchase alone, try to wait longer and save the necessary funds to buy it on your own.

Depending upon the type of construction and property location, at the time of this writing, entry-level industrial buildings range from $500,000 to $1,000,000 for a 5,000 square foot building, and banks typically require about 40% down for an investor buyer loan. So, assuming an average property price of $750,000, that means you need at least $300,000 cash, or exchange real estate equity, for a down payment.

If you have more than that to invest, you can consider larger buildings or multiple smaller ones. However, if this purchase will represent a major portion of your investment portfolio, it is best to avoid a large single-tenant building, because of the vacancy risk. It would be better to acquire two or three small buildings. Granted, that means more management, but your vacancy risk will be diversified. This is particularly important if you are financing the purchase, because, when the building is vacant, you don't want the pressure of having to make a loan payment to affect your discernment in evaluating prospective tenants and negotiating lease terms, or to cause you to lose sleep. In simple terms, it is difficult to be rational if you are being chased by an alligator.

3. Finding a Property to Buy

The location of a prospective purchase property is of primary importance. It should optimize leasing and resale marketability, tenant security, and long-term value stability. The broader area should have residential communities and diversified commercial industries that create demand for products and services from businesses that need the type of lease space provided by the prospective purchase property. You should not invest in a property that is located in a "company town" or an area that is economically dependent on one industry, because if that company or industry goes into decline, the rental market and property values will too.

Accessible locations with high drive-by traffic counts increase the lease marketability of properties, because they provide the lessee with signage advertising benefits. (The terms "lessee" and "tenant" will be used interchangeably in this book, as will the terms "lessor" and "landlord.") Corner properties are particularly desirable, because they have sign exposure on two streets.

On-street parking availability is also of value, because it allows lessees additional customer and employee parking beyond that provided on site.

Some cities have Economic Development Zones that offer employers tax incentives to locate there, which benefits tenant businesses and, consequently, increases the marketability of properties located in such zones.

Relatively safe geographic areas for industrial real estate are around major airports and in metropolitan industrial parks. As a starting point in your search, you might drive around such areas and look for "For Sale" or "Available" marketing signs and contact the offering party for details. The following approaches are also useful:

A. "LoopNet" is a national commercial real estate multiple listing service that can be accessed by the public. The website allows you to search for commercial property for sale or lease, by type, size, amenities, and location.

B. View the websites of commercial real estate brokerage companies in your geographic area of interest. Most will present their listings of available properties.

C. Many title companies provide real estate agents with "farming packages," which list the names and addresses of the property owners in a specific geographic area. The agents then use this contact information to canvass and cultivate client listings. Likewise, you can obtain a farm package for your geographic areas of interest and then mail personal letters to the industrial building owners, inquiring if they would consider selling. This is not a particularly efficient approach, but it can yield some positive results. For example, you might get a response years later when the owner is ready to sell. Farming packages can be acquired through title company websites or by calling their customer service departments, and there is usually no charge.

4. Evaluating a Prospective Property's Economic Feasibility

Once you have located a prospective purchase property, the next step is to evaluate its economic and physical characteristics. To evaluate a property's economic feasibility, it helps to understand "cap rates" and "cash-on-cash" return calculations, and lease terms.

A. Understanding Capitalization Rates (Cap Rates)

People invest to receive a return. Expressed as a percentage, that return on investment is calculated by dividing the investment's net annual income by the amount of capital invested. That resulting percentage is called the investment's "capitalization rate," commonly referred to as its "cap rate." Cap rates are set by the marketplace as a reflection of the risk of the investment, and are used to compare different types of investments. For example, federal government bonds and blue-chip stocks might have cap rates in the 2% to 3%

range, whereas investing in the purchase of a restaurant or clothing-store business might have a 10% to 15% cap rate. Put simply, the higher the risk, the higher the cap rate. Industrial building cap rates tend to range somewhere in between 5% and 12%, depending on the vacancy factor of the area and the particulars of the subject property. Consequently, it is important to know the prevailing cap rate of properties in the geographic area in which you wish to invest.

To ensure that you do not overpay for a prospective purchase property, it is necessary to calculate its cap rate and compare it to the prevailing local market cap rate. If the prevailing cap rate is higher, it means that the asking price of the prospective purchase property is too high relative to its net income, in which case you need to negotiate a lower purchase price.

The following is an example of how to calculate a property's cap rate:

The prospective property's asking price	$1,000,000
Gross annual rents	$88,333
Annual operating expenses:	
Taxes	$12,000
Insurance	$1,000
Maintenance	$1,500
Management fee	$4,416
Vacancy factor	$4,416
Total expenses	<$23,333>
Net annual income	$65,000
Cap rate	$65,000/$1,000,000 = 6.5%

When marketing an income property, some sellers do not include management or vacancy factor expenses in the calculation of the property's represented cap rate. The above example uses a 5% vacancy factor and a 5% management fee. If these were omitted, the net income would be increased to $73,833, which would increase the cap rate to 7.38%, which would make the property more desirable to investors, and therefore more marketable. So, clearly, it is very important to check the reality of the expenses used in the represented cap rate calculation.

Every type of real estate investment has a typical range for its particular operating expenses, expressed as a percentage of gross rental income. For example, industrial property management fees typically range from 3% to 7%; vacancy factors typically range from 4% to 10%; and there are similar expense percentage ranges for janitorial services, utilities, security, taxes, insurance, landscaping and general maintenance, and so on. When buying an investment property, it is imperative that the investor and his or her agent have good knowledge of these expense standards in order to rely on the expense figures underlying the annual net income in the cap rate calculations.

If the prospective purchase property is vacant, the cap rate calculations must depend on estimated lease rates based on historical or asking lease rates for comparable properties in the same geographic area, referred to as "proforma" calculations. "Comparable properties" are those of similar age and physical characteristics and location.

B. Understanding Cash-on-Cash Return

If you plan to finance the purchase of a property, you should first consider its "cash-on-cash return," which is expressed as a percentage. It is calculated by taking the property's net annual income and subtracting from it the annual debt service (loan payments). The resulting amount is then divided by the loan down-payment amount. Using the above example, assume that the purchaser put down $250,0000 cash and obtained a purchase money loan of $750,000 at 6.5% interest amortized over 30 years. The investor's resulting annual loan payments would be approximately $57,000. Subtracting that amount from the net annual income of $65,000 leaves $8,000 in cash flow. The resulting cash-on-cash return calculation would be as follows:

$8,000/$250,000 = 3.2%

You then need to consider if the indicated cash-on-cash return is adequate, compared to the potential return offered by alternative investment opportunities.

C. Evaluating a Property's Lease Terms

Beyond the cap rate consideration, it is important to investigate the property's existing tenant leases, because their terms will have a direct financial impact on you. Industrial building leases are typically "triple net" or "gross." Triple net leases (also referred to as "NNN") are so named because the lease income the lessor receives is net of property taxes, maintenance, and insurance expenses—which the lessee pays, in addition to the monthly rent.

Under gross leases, the lessor typically pays the property taxes and insurance, and the lessee—in addition to the rent— pays for the maintenance of the property. This can vary in many respects. For instance, some multitenant building leases require the lessor to pay the common-area maintenance while others impose a common-area maintenance fee on the lessees. Some gross leases require the lessor to maintain the roof, foundation, and bearing walls, while others require the lessee to maintain the property in all respects. Lease terms also dictate how the expense is allocated between lessor and lessee if a major property component (e.g. HVAC systems, water heater, parking lot asphalt) fails and must be completely replaced, as compared to just maintained.

Knowing the remaining term of the lease is important. If the lease expiration date is approaching, you might request as a condition of the purchase that the lease be extended at terms acceptable to you. If the lease grants the lessee options to continue to lease or purchase the property at certain terms, you need to make sure those conditions are in your economic best interest.

There should be an adequate lessee security deposit to cover the cost of any deferred lessee maintenance and cleanup expense at lease-end. Particular attention should be given to who the lease designates as the lessee. If the business is a "C-Corp" or LLC-type entity, or just a "doing business as" (DBA) company, I prefer to have the principal of the C-Corp or LLC, or the owner of the DBA company, also on the lease as an additional lessee; otherwise, there might be no source of compensation to sue if the company fails or the C-Corp or LLC declares bankruptcy. And I prefer that the lessee's principal or business owner have his personal residence (with substantial equity) in the county or same court jurisdiction as the prospective purchase property; otherwise it is difficult to lien such property with a court judgment.

D. Evaluating a Tenant's (Lessee's) Credit

In addition to considering the property's cap rate, cash-on-cash return, and lease terms, it is imperative to evaluate the lessee's creditworthiness, which requires reviewing the lessee's financial statements and income tax returns, and running a credit check on the principal. This is covered in detail in **Subject 30: Qualifying a Prospective Tenant (The Financial Colonoscopy)** and **Subject 53: Reviewing a Prospective Tenant's Financial Statements**.

5. Evaluating a Property's Physical Characteristics

After you confirm that the prospective purchase property is economically feasible, based on its cap rate, cash-on-cash return, and lease terms, the next step is to evaluate its physical characteristics, starting with age. Obviously, newer is better, maintenance-wise. However, an older building can still be viable if it has been properly maintained.

The two most common styles of industrial building construction are concrete "tilt-up" and metal "Butler." Steel has the highest strength-to-weight ratio of any building material. Therefore, steel creates a stronger building with less material and cost than concrete. The roofs of metal buildings are easy to maintain and durable. Most older tilt-up buildings have "built-up membrane" roofs which are composed of layers of tar, tarpaper, and aggregate. Newer tilt-ups have membrane roofs made of synthetics (EPDM, CPO, etc.), which handle temperature change and resist corrosives well. In my experience, metal roofs offer the best performance.

The next characteristic is land coverage. A general purpose industrial building typically has about a 30% to 35% building-footprint-to-land ratio, which allows adequate room for property line setbacks, landscaping, parking, and a yard area. More land is better than less, but if you are paying for extra land in the purchase price, you will need to charge more in rents to justify it, which means you must find tenants who are willing to pay a higher rent because they need extra land, which will limit your prospective tenant base, marketing-wise.

General purpose industrial buildings typically have 10% to 25% of their square footage built out with air-conditioned office space, which usually consists of a reception area, some private offices, office restrooms, and a warehouse restroom. Buildings with more or less than the above-stated office area limit the market base for leasing. Office interior finish usually includes fluorescent lighting, window blinds, a wet bar, carpeting, and vinyl flooring in the restrooms.

Buildings usually have a 14 ft. to 20 ft. ceiling clearance, with ground-level truck doors. If the building exceeds 5,000 square feet in size, most construction codes require it to be fire sprinklered, which is a marketing benefit, because it can accommodate a broader range of tenants. However, sprinkler systems are also problematic in that they require expensive monitoring systems and periodic fire department inspections.

Other beneficial building amenities include warehouse skylights, security systems, high-speed communications wiring, 200 to 400 amp / 240/480 volt power panels, warehouse power distribution, warehouse wall insulation (in metal buildings), fenced yard areas, and extra land for additional parking and semi-trailer truck turnaround.

6. Negative Physical Characteristics and Undesirable Tenants

Avoid multitenant buildings that have common-area parking, landscaping, restrooms, utilities, and so on, because you will be responsible for maintaining the common area and paying the common utilities, such as water and trash collection. Even if you charge the tenants a pro rata common-area maintenance fee, such properties still create management problems. For example, if someone abandons barrels of spent oil on the driveway, or dumps tires or other trash on the common area (and believe me, that happens), the tenants are going to call you or your property manager to take care of the problem. It is far better to have a single-tenant building in which the tenant is responsible for all the maintenance.

If you do choose to purchase a multitenant property, 5,000 square feet or larger tenant units are better than 1,000 to 2,000 square feet incubator size, because smaller tenants tend to be startup businesses, which either fail or outgrow the space quickly, which means more turnover, cleanups, and management headaches.

Avoid properties that have above or underground chemical storage tanks. Leakage from such tanks is common, and the cost of tank removal and soil remediation is costly. Also, make sure the seller discloses any history of hazardous materials contamination, and provides evidence of proper cleanup.

Avoid properties with unique uses, such as churches, gymnasiums, indoor shooting ranges, and so on, or that have special-purpose improvements, such as cold storage rooms or dropped ceiling manufacturing/assembly rooms, because they will limit marketing the space to the broadest possible range of prospective tenants.

Avoid properties with tenants who process or store large quantities of hazardous materials. Aside from the cost of cleanup if the tenant defaults on the lease, you must disclose to prospective tenants, buyers, and insurers the fact that the property had previously been contaminated, which will interfere with leasing, selling, and insuring the property in the future. If a tenant uses or stores small quantities of hazardous materials, such as pest control, cleaning, or petrochemical products, make sure that they are using methods of handling and storage approved by the Occupational Safety and Health Administration (OSHA).

Avoid properties with tenants doing automotive repair. They expose the property to petrochemical contamination, stain warehouse floors, and get grease marks on office and restroom walls and flooring. Also, if the business fails, the property owner might find himself stuck with a yard full of abandoned, inoperable vehicles, and he will have to pay to clear their titles and dispose of them.

Avoid properties with tenants who, by virtue of their business, accumulate waste materials or throwaway items. If such tenants fail, the property owner might find himself stuck with a yard or warehouse filled with old tires, scrap carpet, demolition debris, barrels of spent industrial fluids, traded-in appliances, and so on, and he must pay to have it all removed and disposed of.

7. Making the Offer to Purchase

There are adequate standard forms available for this purpose, but in summary, the offer to purchase can be in letter form, dated, and addressed to the seller or his agent. It should make reference to the property by address; state your offered amount; state any conditions of the purchase, such as financing and inspection contingencies and the period of escrow. It should also state that the offer is not binding until a formal purchase and sale agreement has been executed by the buyer and seller, after which escrow shall be opened and a good-faith deposit made; and it should have a closing paragraph stating that the offer shall expire in a reasonable number of days, depending on the circumstances.

Properties are often priced around 10% higher than the amount at which the seller is willing to settle. So, the primary purpose of the offer, also called a "letter of intent to purchase," is to express your interest in purchasing the property and open a dialogue to negotiate the price and other particulars.

8. Negotiating

Know the market conditions. Common sense dictates that if there are many similar buildings available and few buyers, you should offer less than the seller is asking.

Understand the seller's motivation in selling. If he needs the sale proceeds quickly and you have all cash, you might agree to a short escrow for a lower price. Conversely, if he is retiring and his business occupies the property and he needs to lease back the building until he winds down his business or finds a buyer for it, you might achieve a lower purchase price by accommodating his transition needs.

Regarding the "good-faith deposit," it should be an amount adequate to assure the seller that you are serious about the purchase, but do consider that it will be forfeited to the seller as liquidated damages if you fail to perform without reasonable cause.

Assuming market conditions allow it, **always counteroffer for better terms**. Counteroffering for better terms is simply a matter of putting a few words on paper or passing some air across your vocal cords, and by doing so, you can save yourself thousands or millions of dollars.

As additional terms of the purchase, you might request that the seller perform property cleanup or deal with maintenance items, or contamination mitigation, or make certain improvements. However, if the property meets your needs, in general, do not permit minor points to spoil the overall negotiations. As the old saying goes, "Don't let the tail wag the dog."

Always be prepared to walk away from a bad deal. Stay objective. Do not allow your anxiousness to acquire a property to cause you to acquiesce to unfavorable terms.

Be patient. Do not allow yourself to be rushed into a decision. Likewise, allow the seller adequate time to consider your offered terms. The quickest way to lose a trout is to set the line drag too tight and try to force it in.

Understand that in all business negotiations, time is of the essence. Once agreement has been achieved, promptly conclude the transaction. **Delays in closing a deal invite failure.**

Above all, be polite and ethical, and always perform on your commitments. The ideal transaction should be a win for both parties.

9. The Purchase Agreement

After price and other major terms have been agreed to in the offer/counteroffer stage, the next step is to execute a definitive "purchase agreement." Though not necessary at this point, it is certainly efficient to contact a reputable title and escrow company, such as First American or Chicago Title, ask to speak with an experienced escrow officer, and obtain an "escrow number" to reference in drafting the purchase agreement.

Standard purchase agreement forms are available through the websites of professional real estate associations such as AIR CRE, the Society of Industrial and Office Realtors (SIOR), and the California Association of Realtors (CAR). Such forms are comprehensive and self-explanatory, and most also serve as "escrow instructions." They are relatively expensive, but not as costly as having a real estate attorney draft custom documents, which is not generally necessary unless there is unusual legal complexity to the transaction. If you employ a commercial real estate agent to represent you in the purchase, they should provide and complete the proper forms as part of their representation service.

As conditions of the purchase, I usually request the following:

A. That the seller prepares a standard form, non-residential "Property Information Sheet," which will state the seller's "disclosures" regarding any known or suspected property defects or other conditions that could negatively impact the use or value of the property.

B. That the property's existing tenants (lessees) prepare and deliver into escrow an "estoppel certificate," attesting that the lease is in full force and effect, the amount of security deposit being held by the lessor (which should be credited to your escrow account), and that the seller (lessor) is in current compliance with his lease obligations.

C. That the property be inspected for physical defects and deferred maintenance. If there is substantial deferred maintenance, I review the lease to determine whether it is the lessor's or lessee's responsibility to cure. If it is the lessee's, I get a written acknowledgment of that responsibility from the lessee, and confirmation that they will fulfill that obligation, and make sure that the lessee's security deposit is adequate to cure such deferred maintenance if the lessee fails to do so. If it is the lessor's lease obligation and if it would pose a breach of the lease if the lessor did not perform, then I have the lessor perform such deferred maintenance as a condition of closing escrow, or credit my escrow account with the funds necessary to perform said deferred maintenance.

Depending on the nature of the property, I might have a surveyor confirm the property lines and make sure that there is no encroachment onto neighboring properties, and that neighboring properties are not encroaching onto the subject property.

If there is reason to suspect that the property might have been contaminated with hazardous substances, I request a Hazardous Substance Conditions Report, which also reveals any contamination history of adjacent or nearby properties — because underground contamination can migrate in a plume that crosses property lines.

Most of the standard purchase agreement forms available through the abovementioned commercial real estate associations have optional-use paragraphs to accommodate the above suggestions.

Once the purchase agreement is prepared, the next step is to sign it. Time is of the essence for all business transactions, and for real estate transactions in particular. So, when it comes to executing contracts or agreements of any kind, I normally include a clause stating that if the other party fails to execute and return the document to me within a certain time limit, it will be deemed null and void. And I always have the other party sign first, which allows me to maintain the final decision as to whether the transaction should proceed or not.

10. Opening Escrow

My first commercial real estate transaction in 1977 was representing a client in selling his 22-unit apartment building and purchasing a 25,000 square foot industrial building, in a 1031 tax-deferred exchange. My only previous experience with "escrow" was when my wife and I bought our first home, which was primarily handled by the sales staff of the home developer. Consequently, I was very apprehensive about how to go about opening my first commercial real estate escrow. So much so that I offered one of the senior Grubb & Ellis agents a small portion of my commission if he would help me open the escrow. As it turned out, the process was very easy—if you get an experienced escrow officer.

In summary, the steps are as follows:

A. Contact a reputable title and escrow company, ask to speak with an experienced escrow officer, and set an appointment to open escrow.

B. When you meet with the escrow officer, provide them with an executed copy of the purchase agreement, contact information for you and the seller, and a check for the "good-faith deposit."

Because most formal purchase agreements also include the escrow instructions, the escrow officer need only prepare supplemental instructions that reference the purchase agreement and state the escrow and title company's fees and conditions of service, a copy of which will be sent to you and the seller for endorsement.

Typically, the escrow fee is shared equally by you and the seller. Incidental fees and taxes are borne by you or the seller, depending on the custom in the geographic area in which the property is located, on which the escrow officer will advise you.

11. Contingencies

The escrow instructions should state conditions upon which you may terminate the purchase if they are not fulfilled to your reasonable satisfaction. Such "contingencies to closing" might include the following:

A. Securing a purchase loan (if necessary).

B. Requiring the seller to disclose any known or suspected defects to the property.

C. Reviewing and approving the seller's disclosures.

D. Inspecting the physical condition of the property.

E. Obtaining a Hazardous Substance Conditions Report and "soils inspection," if necessary.

F. Determining if the property is in compliance with all government approvals for its intended use.

G. Obtaining and approving a preliminary title report and obtaining a commitment for standard or American Land Title Association (ALTA) title insurance. You need to inform the escrow officer as to whether you want a standard title policy (which is paid for by the seller) or an ALTA policy, which is normally paid for by the buyer and provides greater coverage as to unrecorded matters that might affect title, and which includes a physical inspection of the property and confirmation of the property lines. For commercial real estate transactions, it is advisable to get an ALTA policy. If purchase of the property requires lender financing, the lender will require an ALTA policy.

H. **Reviewing the preliminary title report in detail is very important**, because it will list any encumbrances, liens, or clouds on the property title, and indicate any easements. If there are any liens or clouds on the title, the seller needs to remove them prior to the close of escrow, which might require paying off loans or civil litigation judgments. If there are easements, you need to read the text of the easements and see them expressed on a site map to determine what impact they might have on your use of the property. The preliminary title report also reveals any covenants, codes, and restrictions (CC&Rs) affecting the property deed, which are very important to read and understand completely, as they affect the permitted uses of the property.

I. Reviewing and approving existing leases and tenant estoppel certificates.

J. Though not a contingency of purchase unless you are financing the property, you should also be lining up your property and liability insurance at this point, to have it in place for the close of escrow. Property and liability insurance is a necessity. NNN lease forms require the tenant to carry such insurance on the building and to also carry their own personal property and liability business insurance. I prefer a gross lease form in which the owner carries the property and liability insurance. Because it is my property that is being insured and I am the one at risk, liability-wise, I want to make sure the insurance is proper and that the premiums are paid. Most lease forms require the tenant to pay the deductible in claims and any increases in the annual premium that occur over the lease term.

Many insurance companies use construction cost data and algorithms that overstate the property's realistic replacement costs, thereby driving up the premium. I have argued this point on multiple occasions and found that some companies will accept an "agreed value" replacement cost. If you are going to take this approach, make sure the agreed replacement cost includes demolition and code upgrades, and that the amount is supported by an estimate from a qualified, local builder.

Some insurers offer attractive initial rates, but impose sizable increases on the annual renewals. If the premium increases are beyond the prevailing rate of inflation, have your agent shop the market for alternative quotes.

I always carry an umbrella liability policy in the multimillions that enhances the basic policy coverage, particularly in the area of "personal injury." I cannot emphasize enough that you should **read and understand every word of your property, liability, and umbrella policies, particularly the exclusions**. Do make sure that vandalism and glass breakage is covered. I had several 8 ft. by 4 ft. street-frontage windows shot out by vandals. They cost $1,000 each to replace—which the insurance covered. I've also had fences hit by vehicles; holes cut in the sides or roofs of buildings to burglarize them; fires; broken-pipe flooding; landscape palm trees stolen; and more. So, proper insurance is a necessity.

The success of the purchase (or any business transaction) is directly dependent on your attention to detail, timeliness, and management skills—you must manage the purchase. **It is imperative that you ride herd on everyone.** To that end, I strongly recommend that you create a calendar of activities that are to be performed by you, the seller, the escrow officer, and others, such as brokers, lenders, appraisers, inspectors, lawyers, tenants, and so on. The purchase agreement and escrow instructions will delineate actions that need to take place by certain dates, and that, if not performed, will result in the termination of the escrow and purchase. Two or three days before an action is required, I send an email to the obligated individual or parties reminding them of what is required, and I confirm with the escrow officer that the act has been performed. If not, to keep the purchase agreement from failing, it might be necessary to draft an "amendment to escrow" granting more time to perform a particular act.

12. Relieving the Loan Contingency

In effect, lenders become your partner in ownership of the property, which violates Rule Number One—avoid partners. But, unless you were born rich or have owned properties long enough to accrue substantial exchange equity, you are probably going to need a commercial loan to purchase your first industrial building. So, commercial lenders are a necessary evil.

Before approaching commercial lenders, I find out if the seller would be willing to provide the financing, which is referred to as "carrying-back paper." If so, the process is much easier than a commercial loan. For one thing, you don't need an appraisal, which saves money and time. You and the seller simply need to agree on a fair down payment, this being an amount that fits your budget and is enough to assure the seller you will not readily default on the loan. Then, you must agree on the interest rate and loan repayment term. Most escrow officers will provide a standard loan "note" form and, at the close of escrow, record a trust deed for the seller, securing the loan as part of their service.

Processing a commercial real estate loan is far more complex than seller financing. First, you must qualify as a borrower, which means submitting your personal financial statements and income tax returns for lender review, plus having a favorable credit check outcome of your loan payment and litigation history. And the property must appraise at a value to support the amount of loan desired, and you must prove that the property will produce enough income that after covering the property-related expenses and loan payments, there is adequate remaining cash flow, which is covered in detail in **Subject 15: The Loan Amount**.

The loan note and trust deed documents used by most commercial lenders are brutally one-sided in their printed language and terms, and they invariably will not modify them. If you achieve a level of real estate ownership at which the lender needs your business more than you need their loan, only then will they exercise some flexibility in modifying the document language.

With lenders, as with other participants in the purchase process, it is imperative that you ride herd tightly on them. Lay out a schedule of milestone dates with your loan officer, such as those for loan application submission; appraisal; escrow loan contingency compliance; loan committee approval; and funding. Prior to each scheduled step, email your loan officer a reminder and then confirm that the item was successfully completed.

I purchased my first industrial building in 1984 at a price of $467,000. I shopped lenders, and the best I could find was a loan of $300,000, at 3.25% over the 11th district cost of funds (which equated to a 13% interest rate), adjustable every five years and amortized over 30 years. I had $100,000 to put down, so I asked the seller to carry back a loan of $67,000 for five years. The lease income barely covered the debt service and expenses. Was it worth the risk? I sold that 11,000 square foot building 20 years later for $1,134,000 and exchanged it into three newer buildings that are now worth in excess of three million dollars—all clear and free. The point being: Though lenders are undesirable partners, sometimes they are necessary to get ahead.

Aside from enabling you to buy properties, there are two additional benefits to loans:

A. Inflation helps pay them off. Assuming you have a fixed interest rate, which most loans do, the amount of your monthly payment remains fixed over the life of the loan. But, thanks to inflation, your rental income rises— providing more money (inflated dollars) to make the loan payments.

B. Inflation increases your equity position. For example, if you bought a building for $1,000,000 and had a loan of $700,000, you would have only 30% equity in the property ($300,000/$1,000,000 = 30%). In 20 years, thanks to inflation, the building might be worth $2,800,000. Assuming for simplicity you made no payments, the loan balance would still be $700,000. But, thanks to inflation, your equity in the property would now have increased to 75% ($2,800,000 - $700,000 = $2,100,000 equity, divided by $2,800,000 = 75%). In reality, it would be even more, because you would have paid down some of the loan balance. This is one of the reasons the Federal Reserve vehemently fights to control inflation—to protect commercial lenders from devaluation of the loans they make.

Purchase loans might be necessary to grow your industrial real estate portfolio, and some people reason that financing the purchase of a building is justified if investing your capital elsewhere can earn a greater return than the loan interest expense for buying the building. Regardless, I believe that it is best to eventually be loan free, because having a bank as your real estate partner creates complications, and having to make loan payments when you have vacancies can cause you to lose sleep and make bad decisions. **Bottom line, you don't want an alligator chasing you.**

13. Loan Appraisals

In order to secure a loan, the lender will require that the property be appraised—at your expense. The appraisal is going to need to come in at the purchase price or higher in order for you to qualify for the loan amount you have budgeted. To make sure that happens, you need to influence the appraisal in your favor without appearing to interfere with or bias the appraiser — particularly since he will be contracted by or be an employee of the lender. To do that, it helps to understand the appraising process.

14. The Appraising Process

There are three approaches to appraising a property:

A. **"The Market Comparison Approach,"** in which the appraiser determines the subject property's value by considering the recent sales of comparable properties. If the appraiser is doing a thorough job, he must compare the physical characteristics of the subject property to those of each of the comparable properties, and then make value adjustments based on the differences in location (e.g. drive-by traffic signage exposure, freeway proximity, Enterprise Zone tax advantages), age, the amount of land area, office buildout, deferred maintenance, and special amenities, such as heavy electrical power, fenced yard, skylights, solar power, unique landscaping, and off-site parking availability.

B. **"The Income Approach,"** in which the appraiser values the subject property by first determining the prevailing cap rate (i.e. a property's net annual income divided by its current market value, expressed as a percentage) for recently sold comparable properties and then dividing that cap rate percentage into the subject property's net annual income (i.e. rental income minus expenses for property tax, insurance, maintenance, management, and vacancy factor). For example, if the prevailing area cap rate for similar properties is 6% and the subject property produces a net annual income of $42,000, the implied value would be $700,000 ($42,000/6% = $700,000). To be accurate, the appraiser should be confident that the comparable properties' tenant leases reflect current prevailing rent rates.

C. **"The Replacement Cost Approach,"** in which the appraiser values the subject property by estimating the cost to buy and improve a comparably located and sized parcel of land, and adds to that the estimated cost to reconstruct the building, adjusted to reflect the subject property's age and deferred maintenance. Here, the appraiser might rely on recent comparable land sales, industry standard construction costs, and estimates from local builders.

The appraised value is typically a weighted average of the above three approaches, with the weighting dependent on the subject property's characteristics and the marketplace. For example, if there are very few comparable property sales, greater weight might be given to the Replacement Cost Approach. If the subject property has a below-market lease that is expiring soon, less weight might be given to the Income Approach, the calculation of which depends on current net income.

As you can understand from the above, the appraisal result is highly dependent on the appraiser using relevant comparable properties and making proper value adjustments for differences between the subject property and the comparables. To that end, it is in your best interest to gather your own comparables and replacement cost information, and, if your findings support your desired resulting subject property value, you should submit them to the appraiser before he begins the appraisal process.

If you are being represented by an industrial real estate broker in the purchase, he should be able to provide you with comparable sales, cap rates, and replacement land values. You can also obtain comparable sales information, usually free, by contacting the customer service department of your chosen escrow/title company and providing them with the address of your subject property. And you can obtain prevailing lease rate information from local commercial real estate agents, or by searching commercial real estate multiple listing services, such as LoopNet, for comparable properties in the same city as your subject property. For accurate building replacement costs, you should obtain estimates from local commercial property developers and builders.

15. The Loan Amount

Once the lender has the appraised value of the subject purchase property, they will determine how much they will loan, which, for an investor, is typically 50% to 70% of the appraised value. They will then determine if the property's rental income is sufficient to cover its expenses and debt service (loan payments). Some banks use the ratio standard that, after paying property tax, insurance, maintenance, property management and a vacancy factor allowance, the remaining "net annual income" should be enough to pay at least 125% of the debt service, which leaves a comfortable cash flow margin. For example:

Appraised property value	$700,000
Determined loan amount (50%)	$350,000
Annual debt service	$30,000
Annual gross rental income	$49,500
Less:	
Property tax	<$5,000>
Insurance	<$2,000>
Maintenance	<$2,000>
Property management	<$1,000>
Vacancy factor reserve	<$2,000>
Resulting net annual income	$37,500
Less annual debt service (for a loan at	
6% interest/20-year amortization)	<$30,000>
Resulting net annual cash flow	$7,500

In the above example, the ratio of the net annual income to annual debt service is 1.25 to 1 ($37,500/$30,000 = 1.25). So, by that standard, a purchase loan of approximately 50% ($350,000/$700,000) would be approved—subject to the borrower's creditworthiness.

16. Closing Escrow

Escrow is ready to close when all the contingencies are relieved and the necessary purchase funds are deposited. The escrow officer will (A) prorate through the date of the close of escrow the property tax, rents, and any other property-related expenses or income, and post them to the appropriate buyer's and seller's accounts; (B) credit to the buyer's account the tenant's security deposits being held by the seller; (C) prepare a grant deed transferring ownership of the property from the seller to the buyer; (D) prepare a loan trust deed securing any financing; (E) forward those documents to the County Recorder's Office for recording; and (F) they will then provide the buyer and the seller with closing statements detailing their respective account postings, and make any funds disbursements.

17. Constructing a Building

If you prefer to build new rather than buy, you will need to arrange construction and permanent financing (if necessary), buy the land, and hire an architect and a general contractor. If you are energetic, well organized, have the time, and are very hands-on, you can oversee the construction yourself, pulling permits, hiring the tradespeople and services, buying and scheduling the materials, and being on site every day to supervise the work and coordinate inspections.

When I construct a property, because I want to make sure the work has been done correctly, I tell the inspectors to take their time and do a thorough job—which tends to surprise them, because most contractors consider inspectors to be just a bother. Constructing a building yourself is a major task, but it's also very rewarding.

One of the problems with constructing a building yourself is finding a well-located parcel of land that is properly zoned and has all the necessary off-site improvements, such as curbs, gutters, and utility hookups ready. The best source of such land is an industrial park that has already been zoned and subdivided for that purpose. Such developments are usually well planned, relative to supporting demographics, commercial marketplace, and infrastructure. Most such developments also offer a range of building sizes with standard floor plans that can be purchased complete or built-to-suit on vacant parcels. This tends to be the more efficient option than building yourself, time-wise and money-wise, because the developer has the economy of numbers, material, and labor costs, and a team in place to coordinate the parcel purchase, financing, and constructing of the building; plus, in most states the developer is obligated by law to warranty the property to be defect free for some period of time. I have purchased new buildings in such parks, and the relationship with the developer has proven invaluable in resolving post-construction problems, even years after the purchase.

If you take the industrial park developer approach, you will enter into a land parcel purchase agreement and a building construction contract with the developer. Usually, you will need to completely fund (pay for) the purchase of the land parcel, because lenders will not make the construction and permanent (takeout) loans unless you have adequate equity in the project. The project will be "progress funded" from the construction loan, which will be paid off by the takeout (permanent) loan on completion.

18. Finding a Tenant

Now that you have purchased or constructed a building, assuming it is vacant, you need to find a tenant. If you are a hands-on type investor, the following steps will guide you through leasing out the property. If this is your first industrial building and you are not sure you want to "do it yourself," it is best to hire a skilled real estate broker to represent you in marketing the vacant space, finding and qualifying a tenant, negotiating lease terms, and drafting documents. Regardless of whether you hire a broker or not, you should still read and understand the leasing process, because the knowledge will help you oversee your agent's service and optimize your investor experience.

19. Choosing a Lease Format

A. Triple Net Leases

Investors who do not wish to be involved in the management of their property often use a "triple net" lease format, under which the rent received by the lessor is net of property taxes, insurance, and general maintenance—thus the NNN designation, and also simply referred to as a "net lease." Generally, the lessor's only obligation is maintenance of the roof and bearing walls.

Under most such leases, in addition to the rent payment, the lessee directly pays the property taxes, insurance, all property maintenance, and utilities.

B. Gross Leases

Under a gross lease format, the lessor pays the property tax and insurance, and is usually obligated for the maintenance of the roof and bearing walls. The lessee, in addition to the rent payment, is obligated to pay its utilities and maintain the property.

This lease form is particularly useful for multitenant properties, because it is impractical for each tenant to be billed for a portion of the property tax and insurance. I often modify the gross lease form, limiting my obligation to maintain the roof to the first year only.

With the exception of the property tax, insurance, and maintenance paragraphs, both lease forms are similar, starting with the names of lessor and lessee, then the property address and brief description, the period of the lease, the lease rate, and the amount of security deposit.

The lease usually provides the lessee with a warranty period to inspect the property's general condition and test the mechanical systems, such as HVAC, plumbing, lighting, electrical systems, truck doors, and landscape irrigation. If anything is out of order, the lessor is then required to make the necessary replacements, repairs, or maintenance. Thereafter, it is the lessee's responsibility to maintain the property in all respects. If during the term of the lease there is a major failure of some mechanical component that requires complete replacement, it is usually the lessor's responsibility to make such replacements, with a portion of the replacement cost being passed on to the lessee by prorating it over the remining lease term.

Standard lease forms are typically 10 to 15 pages in length and cover a multitude of other items, such as broker commission, attorney fees, late payment charges, subletting, hazardous substances, alterations, damage, destruction, default, breaches, remedies, and more. And there are a multitude of addendums that might be attached, such as "right of first refusal" to continue to lease or purchase, "cost of living adjustment," guarantees, disclosures, and disclaimers.

Similar to the standard purchase agreement forms mentioned in **Subject 9**, standard lease forms are available free through internet sources or for purchase through professional real estate associations. Unless the transaction has very unique circumstances, it is most efficient to use standard forms, because an attorney-drafted lease can be very costly.

Though triple net and gross leases should theoretically net the lessor the same amount, I prefer using the gross form, because I want to make sure the insurance is proper in coverage, because it is I and my property that are at risk. I also want to make sure the insurance and taxes are paid on time, because if a tenant defaults on the lease, I do not want to get stuck having to pay those arrears obligations. For the same reason, at lease-end I withhold the security deposit until the tenant's final utility and service bills have been paid.

20. Determining an Asking Lease Rate

A. Market Comparison Approach

Now that you have decided on the lease type, net or gross, the next step is to determine your asking lease rate, which is usually quoted in dollars per square foot per month or per year, and designated as net or gross.

One approach to determining an asking lease rate is the "market comparison" method, in which you survey the asking or current lease rates of comparable properties, referred to as "comps." Such comps can be obtained by viewing listed lease properties on the websites of local industrial real estate brokerage offices; or by driving around the area, making note of "For Lease" signs on properties similar to the subject property and contacting the offering party; or by doing a search in commercial real estate multiple listing systems, such as LoopNet; or by directly contacting owners and tenants of similar properties in the surrounding area and asking them their current rent rate.

(1) Converting net leases to gross

In considering comp lease rates, the first step is to make sure they are stated in the same lease-type terms as the subject property, that is, net or gross. If you wish to market a building using a gross lease, but the closest comps for that size building are expressed in net lease terms, it is necessary to do a conversion calculation. For example, assume your building is 5,000 square feet in size and has a value of $700,000, and that the closest comp for that size is offered at a lease rate of $0.58/sq. ft./month "net." To convert that net amount to gross, you must add to it an estimated amount for paying the comp property's taxes and insurance, because those expenses are excluded in a net lease rate and included in a gross lease rate. Further assuming the comp has a property value the same as yours, and a property tax rate of 1%/year, the tax would be $7,000 ($700,000 x 1% = $7,000); and assume an annual insurance expense of $1,200, for a total of $8,200. To convert that total to a monthly, per square foot lease rate adjustment, divide it by 12 months, which equals $683/ month; and then divide that by the building size of 5,000 sq. ft., which equals $0.14/sq. ft., which you then add to the comp's asking $0.58 net lease rate, thereby converting it to an equivalent gross lease rate of $0.72/sq. ft./ month. The tax rate and insurance expense used above are arbitrary and for example purposes only.

(2) Adjusting for comp differences

To be accurately comparable, the comps should be located as close as possible to the subject property and be as similar as possible in land size, building size, age, type of construction, improvements, and amenities. If there are substantial differences, it is necessary to adjust the comp's asking lease rate to reflect the differences, which is usually a somewhat subjective estimate. In order to make such adjustments as objectively as possible, it is necessary to know and apply the area's prevailing cap rate to the estimated value of the differing features, then convert that result to a plus or minus, per square foot, adjustment.

For example, assume the subject building is 5,000 sq. ft. in size on a 14,000 sq. ft. site; and that the comp building is also 5,000 sq. ft., but on a 22,000 sq. ft. site, and has an asking lease rate of $0.70/sq. ft./month/gross. In this case you would need to research the value of similarly zoned land located nearby to estimate the value of the comp's additional 8,000 sq. ft. of land. Assuming, for example, your research reveals that such land is selling for $6/sq. ft., the comp's additional land would have a value of approximately $48,000 ($6 x 8,000 sq. ft. = $48,000). Assuming for this example that the prevailing cap rate is 5%, that means that the extra land should yield an additional $2,400 (5% x $48,000 = $2,400) of annual net income, which divided by 12 months equals $200/month, which divided by the 5,000 sq. ft. size of the comp building equals $0.04/sq. ft. as the lease rate value of the comp's additional land. Therefore, the subject property's lease rate should be estimated at $0.66/sq. ft./month ($0.70/sq. ft. minus $0.04/sq. ft. = $0.66), to compensate for the value of the comp's extra land. Similar adjustments should be made, plus or minus, for the value differences in the comp property's other improvements and amenities—such as office space, sprinkler systems, truck wells, and so on.

B. Cap Rate Approach

Another method of determining an asking lease rate is using the prevailing cap rate for industrial buildings in the area of the subject property. For example, if you bought a 5,000 sq. ft. building for $700,000, and the prevailing cap rate is 5%, then the property should produce a net annual income of $35,000 (5% x $700,000 = $35,000). To convert that to a monthly per square foot rate, divide it by 12, which equals $2,917/month, and then divide that by the 5,000 sq. ft. size of the building, which equals $0.58/sq. ft./month, net. If you prefer to use a gross lease, you will need to convert the above calculated net lease rate to gross. To do so, add in the property tax and insurance expenses. For example, if the annual property tax is $7,000 and insurance expense is $1,200, you would divide the $8,200 total by 12, resulting in $683/month, which you would then divide by the 5,000 sq. ft. size of the building, resulting in $0.14/sq. ft./month for the property tax and insurance expenses, which you then add to the $0.58 net lease rate, thereby converting it to an equivalent gross lease rate of $0.72/sq. ft./month.

C. Broker Opinion Approach

Another method of determining an asking lease rate is to ask for the opinion of local industrial real estate brokers, who will often render their professional opinion in hopes of securing a listing to represent you in leasing the property or future business.

21. The Negotiating Cushion

Once you have determined an asking lease rate, I usually add a 5% to 10% negotiating cushion, depending on the market conditions and customs. Some prospective tenants will try to negotiate the lease rate, so it is beneficial to have enough cushion to achieve a mutually satisfying result. However, in a market with many vacancies, you don't want to set the rate so high that you turn away prospective tenants.

22. How Long of a Lease?

Most industrial buildings under 50,000 square feet have initial lease terms of three to five years, with either an option or a right of first refusal to extend. A three-to-five-year initial term provides the property owner with two benefits:

A. It limits your lease commitment, should you decide to sell the property. While the property is under a lease, the only potential buyers are the existing tenant or an investor. If the lease is ending soon, you are free to sell it to an entity ("user") that will occupy it. This is a benefit, because users are generally willing to pay more for a property than an investor.

B. If you must pay a brokerage commission for leasing the property, a three-to-five-year lease limits the amount of commission you must pay. I am quite agreeable to paying a listing or procuring cause broker a commission for the initial term of the lease, but I always put a strike through any wording in listing, commission, and lease agreements that grants brokers a future commission should the tenant extend the lease or purchase the property.

23. Marketing the Vacant Property

After deciding on the type of lease and determining the asking lease rate and lease term sought, the next step is to market the property, which, in a normal market, usually takes three to six months. In a low vacancy rate market, assuming the departing tenant has left the property in proper condition, my transition to a new tenant has always been relatively seamless, time-wise. However, in a down market, finding a new tenant could take many months. In the 2008 Great Recession, I had a building sit vacant for two years.

The following are the steps necessary to market a vacant building:

A. First, I put the property in proper marketing condition. Exterior-wise, the building's walls and windows should be clean and free of any damage. The fences and gates should be in good repair and operational. The parking and yard areas should be clean and free of any debris, and the asphalt should have been resealed and parking spots restriped within the past five years. The landscaping and irrigation system should be in a state of proper maintenance. Interior-wise, the office and restroom walls should be freshly painted or free of any marks or holes, and the carpet/flooring should be clean and free of any stains or damage. The window blinds should be clean and operational. Wet bars, breakroom facilities, office cabinets, restroom toilets, urinals, sinks, and shop utility sinks should be professionally cleaned. The warehouse/shop walls and floor should be clean and free of any damage, and the roof should be watertight. All mechanical systems (HVAC, plumbing, electrical, truck doors, water heater, etc.) should be operational. All office, warehouse, and external lights should be operational. Fire extinguishers should be in place per code; and the property should be in compliance with the American Disabilities Act (ADA) and building code.

The above property preparation might sound excessive, but it is necessary for three reasons:

(1) If it looks good, it will be easier to lease.
(2) It allows you to establish, photograph, and document the lease-commencement condition of the property, in which the lessee will be required to return it at lease-end. If a property is in poor or undeterminable maintenance at lease-commencement, it is likely the tenant will return it in even worse condition.
(3) It helps qualify prospective tenants, because desirable tenants, generally, will not want to lease a poorly maintained property, and tenants that are willing to do so are most likely messy in their business practices and will probably be late with the rent or default on the lease.

B. I place a "For Lease" sign on the property, which has always been the most effective real estate marketing tool, because prospective tenants usually drive around their preferred areas before leasing. I have a sign company prepare a 4-foot by 4-foot, double-faced, brightly colored sign, mounted on posts on the lawn area and positioned for maximum viewing by drive-by traffic. The sign, in bold capital lettering, should say "FOR LEASE" or "AVAILABLE" and state your phone number and the square feet size of the available space. If practical, I also hang a 3-foot by 10-foot, brightly colored "FOR LEASE" banner suspended from the roofline or fencing along the front of the building. In addition to being efficient for finding tenants, signs can save you thousands of dollars in lease commission—if the prospective tenant calls you directly from the sign. If a broker calls from seeing your marketing sign, it is most advisable to be cooperative and assure him that a commission will be paid if he procures an acceptable tenant. It would be a critical error to alienate the local commercial real estate brokerage community.

C. I use my computer word-processor program to prepare an 8½-inch by 11-inch marketing brochure. The top fourth of the page is a bordered photo of the building; the next down fourth is a bordered box divided in half with the left side stating "FOR LEASE" and listing property size and address. The other half is a simple map indicating the property location. The next fourth down is a bordered box listing the property amenities in bullet points. The bottom fourth is a bordered box containing my contact information. Across the very bottom, I print in small type an advisement stating that all measurements are approximate and that all measurements and details should be confirmed by the prospective tenant before leasing. On the back of the brochure, I place reduced-size property site and building floor plans.

D. I place a plastic brochure box and combination lockbox (obtainable at most large hardware stores) on the property's office door, and tape a brochure inside the door glass, so prospective tenants can read the details if the brochure box is empty.

E. I always tape an 8½-inch by 11-inch notice inside the front door, stating in bold capital letters: "AGENTS—PLEASE TURN OFF ALL LIGHTS, LOCK THE DOOR, AND RETURN THE KEY TO THE LOCKBOX WHEN DONE SHOWING." I also tape small signs on the restroom sinks, toilets, and urinals stating, "PLEASE DO NOT USE," to discourage agents and prospective tenants from doing so and leaving them dirtied, which is a marketing turnoff for the next showing.

F. I list the property on commercial real estate multiple listing systems, such as LoopNet; at the time of this writing it is free to do so.

G. I obtain the email addresses of the local industrial real estate agents by viewing the websites of their brokerage firms. I then send an email to each agent informing them of the availability of the property, stating the asking lease rate and that the property is "lockboxed," and to call to obtain the box combination. I attach to the email the Word files for the brochure, and the site and floor plans.

H. I distribute the marketing brochure to the business owners of the tenant companies in the buildings surrounding the subject property. There is an old saying in industrial real estate that if you have a vacancy and stand on the roof and do a 360-degree view, you will probably see your next tenant.

I. I list the property on free internet trade sites, such as Craigslist, and, though expensive and less effective, you might also advertise the property in the want-ads section of the local newspaper.

J. I also email the brochure and cover note to the Economic Development Office serving the area.

24. Marketing a Tenant-Occupied Property

In the event you purchased a property from a seller whose business occupies the property but will soon vacate, or if it is occupied by a tenant that will soon vacate, the marketing procedure is the same as above for a vacant property, with some commonsense exceptions: Though most leases allow you to place a "For Lease" sign on the property and show it to prospects, you should not place a brochure box and lockbox on the property. Ideally, the tenant should be given advance notice of showings, and effort should be made to minimize disturbing their business operation.

25. Handling Leasing Inquiries from Prospective Tenants

When prospective tenants call, they typically first ask, "How much is the rent?" I tell them, but if I am offering the property on a gross lease basis, I ask if they understand the difference between net and gross lease rates, because many do not. This is important because they might be comparing my lease rate to that of other available properties that are quoted as a net lease rate. As explained in **Subject 19: Choosing a Lease Format**, a gross lease rate appears more expensive than a net rate, when in reality it might actually be equal or less. Many tenants do not understand the difference, so I take the time to explain it, because I want them to be comparing apples to apples.

I ask for their name, phone number, and email address for my marketing log. This serves the following purposes:

A. It gives me the ability to send them a brochure and follow up with them later.

B. To qualify for certain beneficial rental property income tax treatments, the Internal Revenue Service (IRS) requires property owners to maintain an activity log to prove that they participated in the management of their property.

C. It establishes a record of my interaction with prospective tenants, in the event a real estate broker makes a claim for a "procuring cause" commission, to which I might not believe he is entitled. Procuring cause can be a tricky area of law. **Good records make for a good defense.**

D. Though the prospective tenant might not be a good fit for my property, I may turn the lead over to property owners or developers I know, to help establish a mutually beneficial business relationship.

It is important to ask prospective tenants qualifying questions to save wasting your and their time, and to avoid making a bad leasing decision. The first question I ask is, "What kind of business do you have?"

- I avoid tenants who process or store large quantities of hazardous materials, because of the potential cost of cleanup if they contaminate the property and default on the lease. Also, if future prospective tenants, buyers, or insurers ask, you must disclose if the property has ever been contaminated, even if it has since been rendered clean. Most tenants do use and store small quantities of hazardous materials, such as pest control, cleaning, or petrochemical products, which are not a problem.

- I avoid tenants who do automotive repair, painting, or body work, because they tend to expose the property to petrochemical contamination, and stain warehouse floors, office and restroom walls, and flooring. And, if they default on the lease, they might leave a yard full of abandoned, inoperable vehicles, which will require the time and expense of title clearance and disposal.

- I avoid tenants who, by the nature of their business, might accumulate waste, trade-in, expended, or demolition materials, such as spent tires, old household appliances or business machines, used carpet and padding, spent processing fluids, and so on. If such tenants default on the lease and abandon the property, the cost of removing such items/materials can be very expensive and time and labor consuming.
- I ask how much space they currently occupy. If the size progression to my building will be more than 50%, I ask why and how they will be able to afford the additional rent.
- I ask how long the prospect has been in business. My rule of thumb is at least two years, and I **avoid startup businesses**, because their risk of failure is too high, unless it is a new branch of an established company.

After the telephone conversation, I send the prospective tenant an email thanking them for the inquiry and restating the property's size, amenities, and lease rate and term, and I attach a brochure, with a site and floor plan.

26. Showing the Property to Prospective Tenants

If the prospective tenant satisfactorily answers my initial qualifying questions, I ask if they would like to see the property. If so, I set an appointment for a showing "as soon as possible," for two reasons:

A. Showing the property and building a personal rapport increases the probability they will lease the property rather than competing spaces.

B. If they inquire about other properties that are marketed by real estate brokers, those brokers will most likely try to secure them as a client and represent them should they decide to lease my property — which means I will have to pay that broker a procuring cause commission. So, it could save you many thousands of dollars if you quickly show your property to and establish a rapport with prospective tenants before they have broker representation.

When I meet for a showing, if the prospective tenant is more than 15 minutes late and does not apologize or offer a reasonable explanation, I politely thank them for their interest and cancel the showing. Their tardiness most likely indicates their character and business habits, which means the rent will probably be late and I will be treated with inconsideration in my lessor/lessee relations. So, it is best to pass on such prospects.

27. Handling Leasing Inquiries from Agents

When commercial real estate brokers or their agents inquire, I employ a similar approach to that with prospective tenants. I get their name, phone number, and email address for my marketing log; I answer their questions about the property, and ask questions to qualify their client. If they ask to show the property, I provide them with the lockbox combination and maintain a log of who intends to show the property on what date, so I can check to make sure the property has been relocked and is in proper condition after their showing. I send them an email thanking them for the inquiry and restating the property's size, amenities, and lease rate, and attach a brochure, with a site and floor plan.

28. Commission

Inquiring brokers are going to ask if you will pay a commission, and probably try to convince you to let them list your property for lease. When commercial real estate brokers represent a property owner under an exclusive listing agreement, they normally charge a commission of about 6% of the total rent for an initial three-year to five-year lease term, and less for longer terms. The broker, referred to as the "listing broker," performs all the above-delineated marketing steps; secures and helps qualify prospective tenants; coordinates lease negotiations; provides forms; drafts, prepares, and delivers offers, counteroffers, and lease documents; and acts as a liaison between the property owner, other agents, attorneys, and prospective tenants. When a prospective tenant is represented by another broker, called the "procuring cause broker," upon consummation of the lease the listing broker splits its commission, 50%/50%, with the procuring cause broker in remuneration for his work in locating a prospective tenant, showing the property, drafting an offer and counteroffers, and doing the legwork to get the lease document executed by his client and delivered back to the listing broker.

Because I market my own properties and perform all of the abovementioned listing broker functions, when procuring cause brokers inquire, I say that I will pay them a 3% cooperating broker commission if they bring in an offer from an acceptable prospective tenant and a lease is consummated to my satisfaction. If, on the other hand, a property owner simply places a sign on his available property and expects inquiring brokers to perform the full services of a listing broker, then he should be prepared to pay a full 6% commission if the broker secures an acceptable tenant.

29. Lease Offers and Counteroffers

If the prospective tenant makes an offer to lease, it will probably be oral, unless they are represented by a broker or attorney. If it is submitted orally or in writing by the prospect, or by their broker or attorney, I send a response letter or email referencing the property address and date of their offer; thank them for their interest; and state my counterpoints to any unacceptable terms of their offer; and state that my counteroffer is nonbinding and dependent on my approval of the prospect's creditworthiness and the execution of a lease document; and that my offered terms, if not accepted in writing by the prospect within some reasonable time frame (I usually say "five days"), shall be deemed to have expired.

30. Qualifying a Prospective Tenant (The Financial Colonoscopy)

After reaching a preliminary agreement on lease terms, I provide the prospective tenant with a "Lease Application" (see **Exhibit 1**), which requests enough information to begin a "due diligence" credit investigation of the prospect's tenancy worthiness. The form requests the following information and documents:

A. Business name, address, phone, email address, and website.

B. The legal entity form (sole proprietorship, corporation, LLC, partnership, etc.). Businesses operating as an LLC or corporation pose risks, because the assets can easily be moved to another vesting entity, leaving nothing to attach in the event of a lease default. Partnerships also pose a risk of failure, because if the partners have a falling-out, the business might not survive. Subsidiaries or branches of larger out-of-town businesses can be a problem, because often there is not a local decision maker, forcing you to deal with an impersonal administration when it is time for lease renewal negotiations or resolving lease problems.

C. The type of business.

D. Years in business. I prefer a minimum of two years in business, as an indicator of stability.

E. Hazardous substance status (handling/storage).

F. The names, home addresses (indicating whether they own or rent), phone numbers, social security numbers, and birth dates of the owners/business principals; and their percentage of ownership. If the prospect indicates that he is "renting" his personal residence, unless there is a good reason, I usually decline to lease. Owning a home indicates financial stability and anchors the individual to the community, and discourages declaring bankruptcy; plus it gives me something to attach with a court judgment if they default on the lease.

G. Bankruptcy and eviction history.

H. Litigation status. If they are being sued, you need to explore why.

I. Annual net income and net worth. Here, I specify, "not gross income." A large gross income means nothing if there is no net income.

J. Copies of current and last year's income statements and balance sheets, and last year's federal income tax return.

K. Current landlord name and phone number.

L. The application requests the signature of the prospect, attesting to the truthfulness of the information provided and granting permission to obtain a credit report and other financial background information, and to contact their current landlord.

Exhibit 1

LEASE APPLICATION

FOR "PROPERTY" LOCATED AT [ADDRESS]

PLEASE COMPLETE AND RETURN TO: Name?

Address?
Phone #?
Fax?
Email address?

PROSPECT'S BUSINESS NAME:_____
( ) Sole Proprietorship   ( ) Partnership
( ) Corporation   ( ) LLC   ( ) LLP

TYPE OF BUSINESS?_____

YEARS IN BUSINESS?_____

DOES THE BUSINESS PROCESS, HANDLE, USE, OR WAREHOUSE ANY HAZARDOUS SUBSTANCES?
( ) yes   ( ) no

PRESENT ADDRESS:_____

PHONE:_____FAX:_____

EMAIL:_____WEBSITE:_____

PRINCIPAL OWNERS OF BUSINESS

(1) NAME OF BUSINESS OWNER:_____

HOME ADDRESS:_____ OWN ( ) RENT ( )

HOME PHONE:_____ SOCIAL SECURITY #:_____

PERCENTAGE OWNERSHIP OF BUSINESS:_____%
BIRTH DATE:_____

(2) NAME OF BUSINESS OWNER:_____

HOME ADDRESS:_____ OWN ( ) RENT ( )

HOME PHONE:_____ SOCIAL SECURITY #:_____

PERCENTAGE OWNERSHIP OF BUSINESS:_____%
BIRTH DATE:_____

HAS BUSINESS OR HAVE OWNERS EVER DECLARED BANKRUPTCY?
( ) yes   ( ) no

HAS BUSINESS OR HAVE OWNERS EVER BEEN EVICTED?
( ) yes   ( ) no

IS BUSINESS OR ARE OWNERS PRESENTLY BEING SUED?
( ) yes   ( ) no

BUSINESS'S AVERAGE ANNUAL *NET* (not gross) INCOME:
$_____

Exhibit 1

BUSINESS'S NET WORTH: $_____

PLEASE ATTACH COPIES OF THE BUSINESS'S:

CURRENT YEAR-TO-DATE INCOME STATEMENT AND BALANCE SHEET
LAST YEAR'S INCOME STATEMENT AND BALANCE SHEET
LAST YEAR'S FEDERAL INCOME TAX RETURN

PRESENT LANDLORD NAME:_____

LANDLORD PHONE #:_____

The undersigned business owner ("Prospect") attests that the above and attached information is true and accurate. The prospect herein gives "Silverwood" permission to obtain credit reports on the business and on the above-listed principal owners. The prospect herein gives its above-listed "Present Landlord" permission to provide "Silverwood" with information regarding the prospect's past rental payment history. The prospect has provided "Silverwood" with the above and has attached information with the expressed understanding that "Silverwood" will hold said information in confidence and use it only for evaluating the prospect for tenancy in the "Property."

PROSPECT:

_____   _____

(1) Owner   Date   (2) Owner   Date

Once I have the completed application and requested information, I then take the following investigative steps:

1. Review the prospect's business website.
2. If the prospect entity is a corporation or LLC, I use a government website to confirm its status, years in business, and obtain the name/address of the contact for service of notice.
3. I contact the customer service department of a major title insurance company to obtain a property profile on the business owner's personal residence to confirm that it is in the same county as my rental property, so I can obtain a judgment lien from a local court if the tenant defaults on the lease; and I want to determine that his residence has sufficient equity, should I need to attach a judgment lien. Property profiles provided by title companies usually include the property address, owner name and address, size, age, purchase price, and purchase loan amount. Ideally, I also obtain property profiles on all properties owned by the prospective tenant business and its owner, so I can lien them, if needed.
4. Review the prospect's previous year's and current year-to-date income statement and balance sheet (see **Subject 53: Reviewing a Prospective Tenant's Financial Statements**); and review their last year's federal income tax return to make sure it reconciles with the financial statements. Accounting expertise is necessary to effectively evaluate a prospective tenant's financial statements and tax returns. If accounting is not your forte, consider having a certified public accountant assist you. If you prefer the "hands-on" approach, read **Subject 52: Understanding Accounting—Everything You Need to Know in a Nutshell**.
5. Run a credit check on the business owner, using one of the big three credit bureaus. The service I use also renders

Exhibit 1

a report interpretation and opinion of creditworthiness. Primary concerns should be a low credit score, late payments, many credit accounts with high balances, or a litigation and bankruptcy history.

6. Contact the prospect's present landlord and inquire as to the prospect's timeliness in rent payments.

7. Access the local county's Superior Court case information website to see if there were or are any civil or criminal proceedings against the prospect's business or the owner.

8. Meet the prospective tenant's business owner in person to judge his appearance and demeanor.

9. Tour the prospect's current business location. If it is unclean and messy, it is an indicator of how he conducts business and how he will perform in your lease relationship. Also, if he stores or handles any hazardous materials, it is important that you see that he is employing proper protocols.

10. Drive by the prospect's personal residence. Like his business, if it is unclean and messy in appearance, that indicates he will most likely mistreat your property and be untimely in paying the rent.

11. Occasionally, a prospective tenant will be a new branch operation of an out-of-state or out-of-country business. In that instance, I use Google Earth to view the facilities of the parent company, to make sure that it is neat in appearance—which I use as an indicator of how they will treat my property and conduct business.

The above due diligence steps might seem like overkill, but a bad tenant can cause immeasurable frustration, lost sleep, damage to the property, attorney fees, and income loss. So, if you do not have the time or desire to do this, consider hiring a reputable private detective to do so, which should cost less than one month's rent, but will help ensure that you will confidently receive the next 36 or 60 months of rent with minimum hassle. **A bad tenant can be worse than no tenant.**

31. Preparing the Lease

Standard lease agreement forms are available through professional real estate associations such as AIR CRE, the Society of Industrial and Office Realtors (SIOR), and the California Association of Realtors (CAR). I recommend the AIR CRE "Standard Industrial Single-Tenant Lease—Gross" form. It is relatively fair in both lessor and lessee protection, comprehensive in terms, self-explanatory, and has easy-to-use "fill in the blanks."

The AIR CRE forms are expensive, but not as costly as having a real estate attorney draft a custom lease, which generally is not necessary unless there are unusual tenant use or legal issues involved. If you employ a commercial real estate agent to represent you in leasing the property, they should provide and complete a standard lease agreement form as part of their listing service.

Though commercial real estate leases are typically 10 to 20 pages in length, it is important to read and understand every paragraph, because they delineate the lessor's and lessee's rights and obligations. When tenant problems arise, and they will, you need to be able to refer to and cite the appropriate lease language in resolution.

Most prospective tenants accept the lessor's lease form without question. However, if the tenant is represented by an attorney or is a major corporation, they might insist on using their own lease form or ask to modify certain provisions of your lease form, which can be a problem. Generally, I refuse to use the tenant's lease or modify mine. However, if the lease is of substantial financial consequence and the lessee threatens to walk if I do not accept their lease form or allow modification of mine, then I might review their form or modifications and make a decision whether or not to proceed, based on my expert knowledge of real estate and law. If your area of expertise does not lie in those fields, you should have a real estate attorney advise you on the legal aspects of their form or modifications; and you should have an experienced industrial real estate broker advise you on the real estate business aspects. **Bottom line, it is better to have no deal than to have a bad deal.**

Completing the standard AIR CRE lease form is pretty easy:

A. First, enter the lessor and lessee names. Most business owners prefer to name their corporation, limited liability company, or sole proprietorship DBA as the lessee, to limit their liability. However, I always try to name the business principal as an additional lessee. It is too easy for a corporation, LLC, or DBA vesting to disappear overnight or declare bankruptcy, which is the reason I prefer that the business principal owns and resides in a home in the same county as my rental property, and that there is adequate equity in the home for me to go after in court if the business defaults on the lease.

B. You next fill in the address and general description of the property. I use the word "approximate" when noting the size of the building. Here, I normally state, "... as described on Exhibit (number?)," which is either the property marketing brochure or a site and floor plan. If this is a multitenant building, it is particularly important to be accurate in your description of the lessee's lease-dedicated area relative to the other tenants' areas and any common areas.

C. Next, enter the term of the lease, and the commencement and expiration dates; then the lease rate and security deposit amounts.

D. The lease asks for a description of the lessee's use of the premises. Be specific here, because it is your means to stop them from later doing something that might be damaging to the property.

E. If it is a gross lease form, it will next ask for the annual base premium for the property's casualty and liability insurance. Though the lessor will be paying the insurance, it is necessary to note the amount because the lessee is responsible for paying any annual increases in the insurance during the lease term. If it is a net lease form, there is no space for the amount, because the lessee will be paying the entire property insurance.

F. Next, the form asks if either the lessor or lessee are represented by a broker, and if so, how much commission will be paid. When I buy, lease, or sell a building, I disclose that I am a licensed real estate broker representing myself only, and indicate who, if anyone, is representing the lessee; and the commission to be paid to that broker.

G. The lease then provides a space for the name of any guarantors.

H. The lease then asks for the descriptive reference of the "Addendums" and "Exhibits" that are attached to the lease.

That is about it for the fill-in-the-blanks. The next 10 to 20 pages of the lease have numbered paragraphs that deal with a variety of important issues, such as maintenance, hazardous substances, default remedies, attorney fees, broker fees, property taxes, and insurance. If not in the printed form, I insert a sentence at the end of the insurance paragraph stating that, in the event of a claim, the lessee is responsible for paying the insurance deductible.

Understandably, lease forms drafted by commercial real estate associations are going to include wording that provides commission protection to brokers. The broker's fee paragraph obligates the lessor and his successors to pay the brokers a commission for all future extensions of the lease, for increases in the lease rate, and for the sale of the building if the lessee buys it. When I was practicing as a full-time broker representing clients, I, of course, wanted those future commission provisions to be part of the lease. However, in my position as a property owner/investor, though I am willing to pay a commission for the initial term of the lease, I will not agree to pay a commission for extensions or if the lessee purchases the property. Consequently, I strike from the broker fees paragraph any provision for future commission, as I also do from any listing or commission agreement I enter into with a broker.

Both lessee and lessor should initial the form in the column alongside any modifications or deletions made to the standard lease wording.

The last page of the standard forms provides signature lines for the lessor and lessee to execute the lease. If, on page one of the lease, a business DBA or corporate or LLC entity has been named as the lessee, and the principal of that entity has also been named as an additional lessee, I make sure to note above the signature line on the final page that he is signing as an officer or owner of the business and as an individual.

I collect the tenant's first month's rent and security deposit on signing the lease. I make a copy of the check for my file, to have the lessee's bank name and account number available, should I ever need to sue them for lease default and attach their bank account to satisfy a money judgment.

32. Lease Addendums

Lease addendums are attached as additional pages to the lease. They add terms to the lease or modify the standard terms. Examples of common addendums include the following:

A. **Cost of Living (COL)** adjustment addendums provide the terms for periodic adjustments to the lease rate to compensate for inflation. A formula is applied using the change in the U.S. Bureau of Labor Statistics Consumer Price Index (CPI) over the adjustment period. In a moderate inflation economy, I adjust the lease rate on a three-year lease at the halfway point (18th month); and every 20 months for a five-year lease. In a high inflation market, every 12 months is appropriate. Standard forms are available for this addendum.

B. **Right of First Refusal (RFR)** to continue to lease addendum, similar to an option, allows a tenant to continue to lease the property for a specified period, but only if the lessor chooses to offer the property for lease to the general public. If not, the lessor has no obligation to continue to lease the property to the tenant and may sell it or occupy it himself. With regard to the lease rate for RFR extension periods, I use the above COL/CPI formula approach to determine the rate, or I reserve the right to determine in good faith a "fair market" extension lease rate myself by surveying the asking and recently consummated rates of comparable properties.

C. **Option to Lease** addendum provides the tenant with the unilateral right to continue to lease the premises for a specified period at a specified lease rate, or subject to a COL adjustment or at a "fair market" rate. Such options benefit the tenant and disadvantage the lessor, because they limit the lessor's flexibility in selling the property. For example, because his financial position might have changed, an investor might wish to sell the property at lease-end. A buyer who will occupy the property (a "user") will typically pay more for a property than an investor. If the current tenant does not want to buy the property, and exercises an option to continue the lease, the lessor must either sell to an investor or wait out the lease extension period to sell to a user. Consequently, I do not grant options to continue to lease. Instead, if the lessee insists on an option, I offer a Right of First Refusal to continue to lease, subject to me continuing to offer the property for lease to the general public. In that manner, the tenant has some assurance he can continue to lease the property and I have the flexibility to take it back at lease-end, should I wish to sell it.

D. **Option to Purchase** addendums delineate the terms by which a tenant can purchase the property during the lease term or at end of lease. Again, such options benefit the lessee only, not the lessor. So, I do not grant them, because such rights complicate marketing and selling the property to other prospective buyers, in that the RFR must be disclosed in the marketing and relieved in writing by the lessee prior to the lessor entering into a sale agreement with others.

E. **Americans with Disabilities Act (ADA)** addendum. There are a multitude of rules, laws, and codes imposing obligations upon business and commercial property owners to provide special facilities and treatment to certain groups of people. Such laws and codes include, but are not limited to, the Americans with Disabilities Act, Title 24 of the California Building Code, and the Unruh Act, generally referred to as "access" laws. Because these rules, laws, and codes are complex and difficult to comply with, thousands of related lawsuits have been filed by disabled individuals against businesses and property owners. Such lawsuits typically also include claims of Civil Rights discrimination violations. Though some such lawsuits are legitimate, many are not. Under the ADA, plaintiffs may file a lawsuit in Federal Court against a business for violations without first giving notice or allowing defendants to correct the alleged violation. Even if a building is in compliance with the ADA and a tenant business does something unbeknownst to the property owner that creates an ADA violation and prompts a lawsuit, the owner can then also be named as an additional defendant in the lawsuit. This creates an untenable situation for property owners, who must either inspect their tenants' business operations every day for ADA compliance, which is impractical; or be constantly vulnerable to ADA lawsuits.

The ADA is so lengthy in text and complex in detail that a formal inspection of any commercial property will virtually "always" turn up a noncompliance, even for a newly constructed property. And, if any violation is found, no matter how minor, the property owner must pay a fine plus the handicapped plaintiff's attorney fees, which can be in the tens of thousands of dollars, even though the attorney is probably using "plug in the name" standardized court-filing documents. Consequently, most property owners and their tenants in such lawsuits acquiesce to paying a ten to twenty thousand dollar out-of-court settlement to the disabled person and his attorney, just to make the lawsuit go away, regardless of whether there was an actual violation or not. It is a very unfair law, so I drafted the following ADA addendum (see **Exhibit 2**), which I include in all my leases, and I have the lessee separately endorse that he has read it and agreed to it. **If you choose to use it, run it by your attorney first.**

Exhibit 2

AMERICANS WITH DISABILITIES ACT (ADA) COMPLIANCE AND LAWSUITS ADDENDUM

To the best of the Lessor's knowledge, the subject premises were constructed in compliance with the ADA and building code access laws in effect at that time. Though the Lessor makes no representations or warranties that the premises are in compliance with all access rules, laws, and codes, he has no knowledge or reason to suspect that they might not be. Nonetheless, the Lessee should conduct its own inspection to make sure the premises are in such compliance. There are special consultants, referred to as Certified Access Specialists (CASp), who conduct such inspections.

If the Lessee's business operations in or modifications to the premises result in a requirement for improvements to be made to conform with the ADA, Title 24, or any other related access rules, laws, or codes, such improvements shall promptly be done by and at the sole cost and expense of the Lessee. The Lessor assumes no responsibility for performing such compliance improvements or related liabilities for failure to do so.

Property liability insurance does not cover defense of claims, fines, settlements, or other costs related to ADA or Civil Rights violation lawsuits. Therefore, if the Lessee's use of or modifications to the premises obstructs disabled access or violates access laws or discriminates against the disabled, thereby resulting in a lawsuit against the Lessor, the Lessee hereby agrees to indemnify and hold the Lessor harmless from all resulting ADA fines, penalties and sanctions, or plaintiff claims for its lawsuit attorney's fees or its damages resulting from personal or physical injury or discrimination; and the Lessee further hereby agrees to promptly (within 30 days of billing) pay for or reimburse the Lessor's lawsuit-related defense costs, including but not limited to attorney's fees, settlements, court costs, and expert witness and consultants' fees. In the event of such lawsuits, the Lessor shall have the right to select his own attorney.

[If you choose to use this form, have your attorney review it first.]

33. Lessee Welcome Letter

Once the lease has been executed and I have the security deposit and first month's rent, I provide the lessee with a key and a "Lessee Welcome Letter" (see **Exhibit 3**). The Welcome Letter is not only a polite gesture; it also serves an important legal and property management function by summarizing the lease warranty provisions and documenting the lease commencement condition of the property.

My Welcome Letter thanks the lessee for their tenancy, advises that the lessee review the lease paragraph that spells out the initial warranty periods for the roof, HVAC, and other mechanical systems, and states in detail the condition of the property and attaches supporting photos. It also provides the names and phone numbers for utilities, phone/cable, security system, and landscape maintenance services.

Exhibit 3

EXAMPLE "LESSEE WELCOME LETTER"

Dear (name of tenant):

Re: (subject property address)

Thank you for leasing my above-referenced property. Herewith I am providing you with keys to the property. You should, of course, have the locks changed for your security.

To the best of my knowledge, all the mechanical systems, such as plumbing, truck doors, lights, and the HVAC, are in proper working order, and the roof membrane is watertight. Nonetheless, you should check everything to your satisfaction. Please read Section 2.2 of our Lease, which spells out the warranty periods for such items, which are in summary: one year for the roof; six months for the HVAC; and 30 days for the other mechanical systems and items.

The building exterior, office and restroom walls, and carpet are clean and free of marks or damage; the window shades are clean and in good operating condition; the warehouse floor is broom clean; all office, warehouse, and exterior lights are operational; there are two fully charged fire extinguishers mounted on the warehouse walls; the fences and gate are free of damage and operational; the yard/parking area asphalt is free of damage and in good condition; and the landscaping is green and properly maintained. Attached is a current set of photos of the property to document its "start-of-lease" condition, in which it should be returned at lease-end.

Exhibit 3

As of the lease commencement date:

1. Please have the electricity transferred to your name by calling (name) at (phone number).
2. Please have the trash collection transferred to your name by calling (name) at (number).
3. Please have the water and gas service transferred to your name by calling (name) at (number).
4. (name) provides the telephone service to the area. Their office number is (number). The building is also wired for cable and internet service (if applicable).
5. I suggest you have a property security system installed and all door and gate locks rekeyed.
6. The weekly lawn/landscaping service is done by (name) at $(amount)/month, which I will have transferred to you for billing. If you see any problems with the landscape, sprinkler system, or weekly cleaning of the grounds, please call (name) at (number). If a sprinkler valve sticks on, there is an irrigation shutoff valve in the planter area by the front office windows.
7. I maintain the property liability/casualty insurance. Please secure liability (naming me as an additional insured) and personal property insurance for you and your business, per paragraph (number) of our Lease.

Your first rent check will be due on (date), which you can send to me at (address).

Thank you for your tenancy. Please call me if you have any questions.

Sincerely,
[Name]

Photo sheet attached

34. Dealing with Maintenance Issues

One of the benefits of owning industrial buildings is that owners have to deal with fewer maintenance problems, as compared to residential and other types of commercial rental properties, because industrial gross and NNN leases require the lessee to maintain the property. Nonetheless, early in the lease, a lessee will occasionally contact me with a maintenance issue, such as, "Water is leaking from a pipe," or, "There is a sewer line blockage," or, "The HVAC is not working," or "There is a roof leak," in which case I politely refer them to the section of the lease that states they are responsible for such maintenance.

Though most property maintenance is the tenant's responsibility, I keep the following list of who to contact for various services, so I can advise the tenant or handle emergencies myself:

HVAC
Plumbing
Roof repair
Asphalt sealing and repair
Landscape maintenance
Locksmith
Truck door
Cement work
Fencing
Window glass replacement
Hazardous material cleanup
Insulation
Gutter cleaning
Carpet cleaning
Handyman
General cleanup

I drive by and inspect my properties on a regular basis to make sure the tenants are performing their maintenance obligations, and particularly if there is a common area that I am responsible for maintaining. On such drive-bys, I have discovered broken windows, dying lawns, graffiti, and other problems the tenant should have addressed. On such discovery, I contact the tenant and advise that they need to correct the problem. If necessary, I cite the lease paragraph that obligates the tenant to do so. I do a follow-up inspection in about two weeks. If the problem has not been addressed, I remind the tenant. Some tenants have the misunderstanding that they need only correct such problems prior to lease-end. In such instance, I explain that it is important to maintain the proper appearance of the property, because a messy property invites vandalism and dumping, and diminishes the desirability of the area and value of the building. If the tenant fails to address a maintenance problem, I have it taken care of and deduct the cost from their security deposit. The next time they want to extend their lease, I require that they first fund the expended portion of their security deposit.

On occasion, the city, county, or utility companies will engage in infrastructure projects such as road work, water supply, sewer lines, and underground cable installations which tear up curbs, sidewalks, and private property landscaping for months at a time, and are allowed because they have an easement to do so. It is a tenant's maintenance obligation to make sure that such agencies return the property to its original condition after such work is completed. However, most tenants do not monitor such work and remediation, because they are busy running their business. If, on a drive-by inspection, I see such work damaging my property or creating a public hazard (such as large holes in the ground, projecting objects, parked excavation equipment, etc.), I take photos and contact the responsible government agency or its contractor with an email advising them that the property needs to be returned to original condition on completion of their work, and that immediate measures need to be taken to ensure the safety of the public. When such work is complete, I inspect the remediation. If my property has not been returned to proper condition, I again contact the responsible government agency or contractor by email with photos of the original condition of the property that were taken at the beginning of my tenant's lease. A well-documented audit trail, with photos, is imperative in resolving this type of problem.

I usually do not make the tenant aware of my involvement in these matters, because I do not want them to think I have assumed that responsibility. And, if the damage to the property is not eventually corrected to beginning-of-the-lease condition, I do hold the tenant responsible for correcting it.

Regarding roof leaks (all roofs eventually leak), if it occurs within my granted warranty period, I provide the lessee with the name of the appropriate contractor and tell them to have the repair work billed to me. And, until it is done, to place a bucket under the leak and cover any water-vulnerable possessions. As I previously mentioned, unless there is a law disallowing it, I modify the standard lease to warranty the roof for the first year only. Thereafter, it is the lessee's responsibility.

If your building has a relatively flat roof and it accumulates leaves, it is imperative that the rain gutters and drains are cleaned every year. Otherwise, thousands of pounds of blocked water can accumulate on the roof in a storm and cause it to collapse.

As to leaking pipes, sewer backups, HVAC problems, and all other maintenance issues, other than bearing walls and foundation, if they occur after the 30-day warranty period they are the lessee's responsibility. Most lessees know this, but they sometimes try to test your ignorance of the lease terms to see if you will do the repair work. So, as I said, know your lease.

There are also odd ones that pop up. I had a tenant call and say that someone had dumped a large pile of trash in the property's driveway. I told him that it was a lessee maintenance matter, that anything that happened to the property during the lease was his responsibility. I said that if someone dumped a pile of gold in the driveway, I doubt he would be calling for me to come pick it up. He did not like it, but he got my point. Same applies to graffiti, broken windows, break-in damage, or damage done to the property's grounds by the city, county, or private contractors doing infrastructure (water, electrical, cable, etc.) work. It is the tenant's responsibility to make such parties repair the damages or repair the damage themselves.

With the above-type tenant interactions, be sure to document your responses by email, fax, or letter, with specific reference to the pertinent lease paragraph. Bottom line, it can be a bit of a struggle with some new tenants, but once they understand that you know and will enforce the lease terms, they eventually assume their responsibilities. Keep in mind that there might be a circumstance where, within the warranty period, the tenant failed to discover a preexisting defect in some mechanical system or other part of the property. Because this can be a tricky area, I exercise fairness in such situations. My general rule is, "Don't let the tail wag the dog," meaning, do not allow a minor expense or questionable obligation to negatively taint a long-term lease relationship.

35. Repairs, Replacements, and Maintenance Service Contracts

Replacements are a different matter than repairs or maintenance. Sometimes a mechanical item is too far gone to repair, so most standard leases have a paragraph to address "replacements."

The AIR CRE form I use says that if the cost to repair an item exceeds half the cost to replace it, then it is the lessor's obligation to replace it. Some leases also apply a formula to add a prorated portion of the replacement cost to the lessee's rent, based on the estimated life of the item in relation to the remaining term of the lease.

Most standard leases have paragraphs requiring the lessee to maintain service contracts on certain mechanical systems, such as the HVAC.

36. Lease Extensions and Amendments

At least six months prior to the lease expiration date, I contact the lessee to see if they wish to extend the lease. If so, I draft an "Amendment to Lease" (see **Exhibit 4**), referencing the lease date, parties, mutually-agreed-to extension term, and lease rate. To determine the lease rate, I often use the same methodology outlined in **Subject 32: B. Right of First Refusal (RFR)**.

Exhibit 4

AMENDMENT TO LEASE

DATED ??
BY AND BETWEEN
name? ("Lessor") and name? ("Lessee")
FOR THE PROPERTY LOCATED AT
address? ("Premises")

Lease paragraph (number?) states a "Lease Term" of (number?) years and an "Expiration Date" of (date?).

Lessee desires to hereby amend the Lease Term to (number?) years and the Expiration Date to (date?); and,

Lessee desires the Right of First Refusal (hereinafter, RFR) to extend the Lease for an additional (number?) year(s), upon expiration of the amended term, subject to the following conditions:

1. That upon expiration of the amended Lease Term, the Lessor intends to offer Premises for lease to the general public.
2. That the Lessee is not in default on any of the Lease terms.
3. That at least 120 days but no more than 180 days prior to the amended Expiration Date, the Lessee informs the Lessor in writing of its intent to exercise said RFR.
4. That the commencing Lease rate for the RFR extension term shall be determined by taking the most recent available U.S. Bureau of Labor Statistics Consumer Price Index for all urban wage earners (hereinafter, CPI) number as of (date?), and dividing it by the CPI number for the Lease Commencement Date of (date?). The resulting fraction then shall be multiplied by the current Base Rent

of $(number?), resulting in the new Lease rate for the RFR extension term.

For consideration, mutually acknowledged as adequate and received, the Lessor and Lessee hereby agree to the above-stated amendment and RFR terms.

ACKNOWLEDGED AND AGREED TO:

LESSOR   LESSEE
(name?)   (name?)
                                By: (print name and
                                       corporate title)

_____   _____

Signature   Date   Signature   Title   Date

[If you choose to use this form, have your attorney review it first.]

If the tenant chooses not to renew the lease, I commence marketing the space at least four months prior to the lease expiration date, using the methods described in **Subject 23: Marketing the Vacant Property**.

Most standard lease forms have provisions that allow the lessor to place marketing signs on the occupied property and to access it for showings. Understandably, I do not place a lockbox on the property, which might compromise the tenant's security. So, to show the property to prospective tenants, it will be necessary to tactfully coordinate with the present tenant to arrange showing times and access. A benefit to marketing a tenant-occupied property is the possibility of a seamless transition between tenants if a new tenant is secured before the current lease expires. Even if you are so fortunate, there is usually at least a 30-day gap between tenants in which cleanup and deferred maintenance must be addressed. On the negative side, the current tenant's personal property, business operations, and deferred maintenance might detract from the building's appearance. Regardless, it is best to get an early start on the marketing, because it could take six months or longer to secure a new tenant.

37. End-of-Lease Letter

If the tenant is not going to extend the lease, one month before the expiration date I tour the property with a site and floor plan and lined writing pad in hand, on which I number, list, and describe in detail every necessary deferred maintenance and cleanup item, and I mark their respective locations on the site and floor plans, referenced to their corresponding list number. I then prepare an "End-of-Lease Letter" (see **Exhibit 5**) in which I thank the tenant for their occupancy, cite the approaching lease expiration date, and state that I have conducted a "preliminary" inspection of the property to determine the deferred maintenance and cleanup they must do to return the property in proper condition at lease-end, and I provide them with a typed list of the items, and site and floor plans showing the locations. Some of my tenants have told me they appreciate having such a list presented, because it makes the task of managing the cleanup easier. They need only give the list to an appropriate staff member and say, "Get it done."

You will notice in my above comments that I said, "preliminary inspection." In my End-of-Lease Letter I ask tenants to try to have the property ready for "final inspection" a few days before lease-end, so they have adequate time to take care of any missed items. I state the amount of security deposit being held and that it will be returned if the property is surrendered in proper condition and if all utility and maintenance service accounts are paid to date. I also attach a copy of the "Lessee Welcome Letter" and commencement-of-lease photos, so the tenant has a clear understanding of the condition in which I expect the property to be returned.

When you do a final inspection, make sure that the required fire extinguishers are in place; that all interior and exterior light bulbs are operational; that all truck doors are operational and undamaged; that all toilets, sinks, and urinals are operational and that there is hot water; that the HVAC is hot/cold operational and that a new filter is in place; that the window blinds are clean and operational; that the office/restroom walls are either free of marks and holes, or freshly painted; that the warehouse floor is clean and free of any oil stains; that there are no holes in the warehouse walls; that the yard area is clean of any debris; that there is no damage to the exterior of the building; that tenant business signs are removed with no damage or potential for rain leakage; that the landscaping is healthy and the irrigation system is in proper working order; that the yard fences and gates are undamaged and operational; that the office and restrooms and windows have been professionally cleaned; and that the office flooring has been professionally cleaned or replaced with new.

The above might seem tedious, but it is worth the effort. My properties are usually returned in excellent condition, costing me very little in time and money to prepare for the next tenant.

Exhibit 5

EXAMPLE "END-OF-LEASE LETTER"

Dear (tenant name?),

Considering that our Lease on the above referenced property expires on (date?), now is a good time to coordinate on return of the property.

The attached Welcome Letter I sent you on (date?) included a set of attached photos memorializing the Commencement of Lease condition of the premises, and it stated in summary:

> "… all the mechanical systems (plumbing, truck doors, lights, etc.) and the HVAC are in proper working order, the roof is watertight, the building exterior, office and restroom walls, and carpet are clean and free of damage, the window shades are clean and in good condition, the warehouse floor is broom clean, all office, warehouse, and exterior lights are operational, the fences and gate are free of damage and operational, the yard and parking area asphalt is free of damage and in good condition, and the landscaping is green and properly maintained."

I have done a limited preliminary inspection of the property and noted below some of the deferred maintenance and cleanup items that you need to do to return the premises in proper condition, per our Lease. I have attached floor and site plans indicating the location of each item, referenced by number to the following list (examples):

1. Replace missing insulation of water backflow valve riser.
2. Clear weeds between buildings.

Exhibit 5

3. Reseed dead spots in lawn.
4. Remove weeds by building.
5. Repair and reattach parking area fence to rear fence.
6. Replace burned-out fluorescent lights.
7. Repair hole in reception wall and repaint.
8. Replace two sets of burned-out fluorescent lights in reception area.
9. In the office restroom, remove loose Pullman sink; and remove wall-mounted telephone wiring panel, and patch/paint wall. Please make sure the sink, toilet, walls, floor, and mirror are clean.
10. Clean office carpet and repaint any marked or damaged office walls.
11. Clean door dirt stains around handles.
12. Patch/paint hole cut in wall, and frame added power plug to code.
13. Clean warehouse sink and backsplash.
14. Clean warehouse restroom sink, toilet, urinal, walls, and mirror, particularly the floor by urinal.
15. Clean both sides of warehouse exterior man-door.
16. Please make sure the office wet-bar sink, countertop, cabinet, and drawers are clean.
17. Dust window blinds and repair any damaged ones.
18. Clean the warehouse floor of dust, debris, and stains. Repair/paint any damage to walls.

I did not have the opportunity to check the exterior condition or operation of the truck doors or to test the operation of the HVAC, water heater, sinks, and toilets, or to check the three exterior security lights—all of which I will do on or before final inspection.

Please try to have the property ready for final inspection a few days before lease-end, so there is adequate time for you to take care of any missed maintenance or cleanup items.

I will refund your security deposit upon receiving the property back in the condition in which you took possession, and when all your property-related utilities and maintenance service accounts are paid in full.

I do not presently have a new tenant for the property. So, if you need to stay beyond (date?) on a month-to-month basis, please let me know.

I appreciate your past tenancy and I wish you continued good health and prosperity.

Sincerely,
[Name]

38. Security Deposit Return Letter

Once I have the property back in proper condition, I wait at least 30 days to return the security deposit, because I want to make sure there are no unpaid utilities or service contract bills — also to allow time to identify undiscovered deferred maintenance items. Thereafter, I send a letter to the tenant delineating any charges against their security deposit, and enclose a check for the net remainder.

39. Early-Termination-of-Lease Amendment

Sometimes leases do not make it to their scheduled end, either because the lessee has outgrown the building and needs more space, or they are having business problems and need less space, or they want to shut down the business. I usually agree to grant an early termination of the lease, subject to me locating an acceptable replacement tenant and the property being returned in proper condition. I then begin marketing the space, and when I secure a new tenant, I draft an early-termination-of-lease agreement that amends the lease. This "Modification to Lease Agreement" (see **Exhibit 6**) references the lease, the lessor and lessee names, the reason the lessee and lessor want to terminate, and the scheduled termination date.

Exhibit 6

MODIFICATION TO LEASE AGREEMENT

This Modification to Lease Agreement (hereinafter, the "Agreement"), dated (date?) for reference purposes, is entered into by and between (name) (hereinafter, "Lessor"), and (name?) (hereinafter, "Lessee"), under that lease (hereinafter, the "Lease") dated (date?) for the premises (hereinafter, the "Premises") located at (address?).

Whereas the Expiration Date of the Lease is (date); and,

Whereas the Lessee has leased another property and desires to vacate the Premises prior to the scheduled Expiration Date of the Lease; and,

Whereas the Lessor wishes to lease the Premises to a new tenant (hereinafter, "name"); and,

Whereas (name?) wishes to take possession of the Premises on (date?);

Now, for consideration that the Lessor and Lessee herein mutually acknowledge as being sufficient and received, they agree as follows:

1. The Expiration Date of the Lease shall hereby be amended to be (date?), with all other terms and conditions of the Lease remaining unchanged; and,

2. The Lessee hereby agrees to indemnify and hold the Lessor harmless from any claims by (name?) or its real estate broker for damages resulting if the Lessee fails to surrender the Premises, per the Lease terms, by (date?); and,

3. This Agreement is subject to and expressly contingent upon the Lessor and (name?) consummating a new lease prior to (date?). If said new lease is not consummated by said date, this Agreement shall be deemed null and void.

Exhibit 6

This Agreement shall be binding upon and inure to the benefit of and be enforceable by the parties hereto, their heirs, successors, and assigns.

ACKNOWLEDGED AND AGREED TO:

Lessee: Lessor:

_____   _____
(name?)   (date?)   (name?)   (date?)

[If you choose to use this form, have your attorney review it first.]

If the lessee has been a good tenant, but is no longer able to pay rent until I secure a replacement tenant, I usually allow the tenant to terminate the lease early if they return the property in proper condition. However, I still execute an early-termination-of-lease amendment, which continues to obligate the lessee in the event that undiscovered property damage or hazardous substance contamination is later found.

It is also possible, via litigation, to try to force such tenants to pay the entire lease obligation or to negotiate an early-termination-of-lease settlement amount, but I do not prefer that approach.

40. Lawsuits

The best way to avoid having to sue tenants is to do a thorough "due diligence" before leasing to them, and, thereafter, maintain a good relationship throughout the lease. The best way to avoid being sued is to be honest, fair, practice attention to detail, read contracts thoroughly before signing, maintain good business records, know the applicable laws, and avoid dealing with people of questionable character.

The time involvement, cost, and stress of a lawsuit is generally not worth the effort, and it's difficult to get blood out of a turnip. So, in the few instances I have had a tenant default on a lease, I have offered to let them off the lease if they leave the property clean and pay any arrears relating to utilities and maintenance bills.

However, if a tenant abandons the property and leaves it damaged and messy; or remains in occupancy but refuses to pay rent; or has been difficult to work with, deceptive, and is clearly trying to take advantage of me, I will sue if my records indicate that they have assets with adequate equity upon which to place a judgment lien and seize.

In such instances, I first file an "Unlawful Detainer" action to regain legal possession of the property; then obtain a judgment for the lost rents and damages to date; then file a "Small Claims" or "Superior Court" action (depending on the dollar amount of damages) for lost rents until the property is re-leased; then place Judgment Liens through the County Recorder's Office on their real properties, and obtain a Writ of Execution for the sheriff to seize their bank account, vehicles, and other personal property.

It is most convenient to have an attorney represent you, but if you have the time and desire, you can do such filings yourself. They are relatively simple fill-in-the-blank forms, many of which can be done online, and there are "process server" services available to serve the documents.

If, on the other hand, you are being sued by a tenant—which I have never been—your commercial liability insurance should provide legal representation to defend you, depending on the nature of the suit.

In the instances where I have had to sue a tenant for breach of lease, or sue a client for nonpayment of commission, I have learned some lessons:

- If deposed, offer just the minimal, accurate answer to the defendant attorney's questions, rather than elaborate on facts and details that support your action against the defendant—because the defendant attorney will then tailor his courtroom arguments to counter or avoid your strong points.
- Even if the defendant is clearly in the wrong and owes you the money, do not be surprised if his attorney files motion after motion to delay trial, trying to get you to become fatigued and go away; and then offers a last-minute settlement (which usually does not cover your attorney's fees), as they say, "on the courthouse steps." The defendant's devious logic here is that if you refuse

the settlement amount, then go to trial and the jury awards you equal to the settlement amount or less, then the defendant can make a claim against you for his attorney's fees. However, if you prevail at trial in your claim or for an amount greater than the offered settlement amount, the court might also award you payment of your attorney's fees and court costs. This is tricky, because you never know what a jury will do. So, you must be very confident of your case to proceed to trial.

- It helps to be aware of court etiquette. Dress conservatively, address the judge as "Your Honor," ask permission to approach the bench, and be well prepared.

41. Selling a Building

Generally, I do not recommend selling your properties, for two reasons:

A. You might incur federal capital gains and state ordinary income taxation on the profits of the sale, which means that portion of your presale equity will no longer be earning income for you. For example, assume you paid $500,000 (your original tax basis) for a property 20 years ago and it is now worth $3,000,000, on which you are earning $180,000/year (6% cap rate) net rental income. Disregarding depreciation, improvements, loans, and sale expenses for example simplicity, your capital gain or profits will be $2,500,000 ($3,000,000 − $500,000 = $2,500,000). Assuming a federal capital gains tax of 20% and disregarding state income tax for example simplicity, you will suffer a taxation of $500,000 (20% x $2,500,000 = $500,000). If you now reinvest your net sale proceeds of $2,500,000 in another building or another type of investment that has a 6% net cap rate, your net annual return will be $150,000 ($2,500,000 x 6% = $150,000), which is $30,000 less than you were earning with your original property, because you lost the earning ability of $500,000 of your equity.

When taking recapture of depreciation and state income tax into consideration, the loss of income-earning equity is even more.

B. It is difficult to find alternative investments to real estate that provide as much stable return. And selling an income property to provide general living funds or to spend on entertainment or toys violates my Second Most Important Rule: "**Never spend your income-producing capital.**"

With that said, and assuming you must sell for a prudent reason, the steps to take are as follows.

42. Determining Your Asking Price

Having a professional commercial real estate appraiser do a formal appraisal is the most accurate approach. However, such appraisals are expensive. So, if you choose to do it yourself, consider the following approaches:

A. **Market Comparison Approach.** Using this method, you survey the asking or recent sale prices of comparable properties, referred to as "comps." Such comps can be obtained by driving around the area, making note of "For Sale" signs on properties similar to the subject property, and contacting the offering party; or by doing a search in commercial real estate multiple listing systems, such as LoopNet; or by contacting the customer service department of a title company, such as First American or Chicago Title companies, providing them with the address and square footage size of your property and asking them to provide a report of comparable properties sales within the past 12 months for properties within a 5-mile radius of yours. There might be no charge for the report if you state that you plan to process the sale through their associated escrow service.

Adjusting for comp differences. To be accurately comparable, the comps should be geographically located as close as possible to the subject property and be as similar as possible in land size, building size, age and buildout, type of construction, and amenities. If there are substantial differences, it is necessary to adjust the comp's asking or historical sale price to reflect the differences. In order to make such adjustments objectively, it is necessary to know and apply the prevailing cap rate to the value of the differing feature, then convert the value to a plus or minus adjustment to your asking price. For example, assume the subject building is 5,000 sq. ft. in size on a 14,000 sq. ft. site; and that the comp building is also 5,000 sq. ft., but on a 22,000 sq. ft. site, and has an asking lease rate of $900,000. In this case you would need to research the value of similarly zoned land located nearby to estimate the value of the comp's additional 8,000 sq. ft. of land. Assuming your research reveals that such land is selling for $6/sq. ft., the comp's additional land would have a value of approximately $48,000 ($6 x 8,000 sq. ft. = $48,000), which should be deducted from the comp's asking or historical sale price to render it as a comparable to your property. Accordingly, the adjusted comp's value would be $852,000 ($900,000 − $48,000 = $852,000). The same type of adjustments, plus or minus, need to be made for other differences in comp properties' components and amenities.

B. **Cap Rate Approach**. Another method of determining an asking sale price is using the prevailing cap rate for industrial buildings in the geographic area of the subject property. For example, if the prevailing cap rate is 6%, and the subject property produces an annual net income of $30,000, the indicated sale value (to an investor) might be $500,000 ($30,000 divided by 6% = $500,000). I parenthesized, "to an investor," because a buyer whose business will occupy the property (a "user") will typically pay more than an investor.

C. **Broker Opinion Approach**. Another method of determining an asking sale price is to ask for the opinion of local industrial real estate brokers, who will often render their professional opinion in hopes of securing a listing to represent you in leasing or selling the property.

43. Negotiating Cushion

Once you have determined an asking sale price, I usually add a 5% to 10% negotiating cushion, depending on the market conditions and customs. Some prospective buyers will try to negotiate the sale price, so it is beneficial to have enough cushion to achieve a mutually satisfying result. However, in a market with many buildings for sale or vacant buildings, you don't want to set the price so high that you turn away prospective buyers.

44. Marketing the Property for Sale

The same steps outlined in **Subject 23: Marketing the Vacant Property** are applicable for marketing a property for sale. Of course, the signs, brochures, and offerings should state "For Sale" rather than "For Lease."

45. Handling Purchase Inquiries from Prospective Buyers

When prospective buyers contact you, usually the first thing they will ask is, "What is the price?" I tell them, but also ask for their name, phone number, and email address for my marketing log, which gives me the ability to send them a brochure and to follow up with them later.

It is important to ask questions to qualify prospective buyers to save wasting your and their time. I ask if they are an investor or will occupy the property. If they are an investor, and plan to finance the purchase, they will typically need 25% to 40% as a down payment, depending on the market. I make that point and ask if that will be doable. If they are a user (i.e. owner and occupier), they can sometimes finance the property with a federally insured Small Business Administration (SBA) loan for as little as 10% down. Though helpful in financing sales where the buyer is cash short, SBA loans add complexities that can slow the transaction, thereby increasing the possibility of failure.

46. Showing the Property to Prospective Buyers

Similar to showing a property to a prospective tenant (**Subject 26**), if the prospective buyer satisfactorily answers my qualifying questions, I ask if they would like to see the property. If so, I set an appointment for a showing as soon as possible, because if they inquire about other properties in the area that are marketed by real estate brokers, those brokers will most likely try to secure them as a client and represent them should they decide to purchase my property, which means I will have to pay that broker a procuring cause commission. So, it could save you many thousands of dollars if you quickly show your property and enter into sale negotiations before they have broker representation.

In **Subject 26: Showing the Property to Prospective Tenants**, I said that I would not deal with a prospect who is more than 15 minutes late for a showing appointment, unless they had a good reason, because such tardiness indicates how they will pay the rent and treat me in future business relations. I am a little more flexible with a prospective buyer's tardiness, because I will not have to deal with them after the close of escrow.

47. Handling Sale Inquiries from Agents

When commercial real estate brokers or agents inquire, I employ a similar approach to that with prospective tenants (**Subject 27**): Get their name, phone number, and email address for my marketing log; answer their questions about the property; ask questions to qualify their client. If they ask to show the property, I provide them with the lockbox combination and make note of the date they intend to show it, so I can check to make sure the property has been relocked and is in proper condition after their showing.

As explained in **Subject 28: Commission**, inquiring brokers are going to ask if you will pay a commission. When commercial real estate brokers represent a property owner under an exclusive sale-listing agreement, they normally charge a commission of about 6% of the sale price for smaller properties, and less for larger ones. The broker, referred to as the "listing broker," performs all the above-delineated marketing steps; secures and helps qualify prospective buyers; coordinates sale negotiations; prepares and delivers offers, counteroffers, and sale documents; opens escrow and acts as a liaison between the property owner, buyer, and escrow. When the buyer is represented by another broker, called the "procuring cause broker," the listing broker splits its commission 50%/50% with the procuring cause broker in remuneration for his work in locating a buyer, showing the property, drafting an offer and counteroffers, and doing the legwork to get the sale and escrow documents executed by his client and coordinated between the seller's agent and escrow.

Because I market my own properties and perform all of the listing broker functions, when procuring cause brokers inquire, I say that I will pay them a 3% cooperating broker commission if they bring in an offer from a qualified prospective buyer that is ready, willing, and able to purchase the property on my terms. If, on the other hand, a property owner simply places a sign on his available property and expects inquiring brokers to perform the full services of a listing broker, then he should be prepared to pay a full 6% commission if the broker secures an acceptable buyer.

48. Purchase Offers and Counteroffers

If the prospective buyer makes an offer to purchase, it will probably be oral, unless they are represented by a broker or attorney. If it is submitted orally or in writing by the prospect, or their broker or attorney, I send a response letter or email referencing the property address and date of their offer; thank them for their interest; and state counterpoints to any unacceptable terms of their offer; and state that my counteroffer is nonbinding and subject to the execution of a definitive purchase agreement; and that my offered terms, if not accepted in writing by the prospect within five days, shall be deemed to have expired.

In negotiating the sale terms, price is primary, but the following buyer's contingencies also require careful consideration:

A. Length of escrow. The shorter the better. The longer the escrow, the higher the probability something will come up to complicate or interfere with the sale. I limit escrows to 90 days or shorter.

B. Sale of another property. I will not enter into a sale agreement that is contingent upon the buyer first selling another property, unless the buyer is in an IRS 1031 delayed closing exchange and has already sold his other property and the exchange escrow is ready to fund my sale.

C. Inspection contingencies are acceptable if reasonable in terms. I usually state in the sale agreement and escrow instructions that, other than my disclosures in the Property Information Sheet, I make no representations or warranties as to the condition of the property; that it is being sold "as is"; and that the buyer should conduct its own inspection.

D. Commercial loan financing contingencies are reasonable if the buyer has the ability to qualify for a purchase loan. Before agreeing to such a contingency, I make sure the buyer has adequate cash to meet a lender's down payment requirement, and I try to limit the period for loan approval to 30 days, but no more than 60.

To expedite the financing process, I provide the buyer with contact information on lenders that loan on properties similar to the subject. I also have comparable sales data ready to provide to the lender's appraiser, to support the agreed sale price.

If I think the buyer can qualify for a Small Business Administration (SBA) loan, which requires only 10% down, I provide the buyer with the contact information for an SBA agent and banks that make such loans. However, unless it is a last resort to make the deal, I try to avoid SBA loans, because federal regulations for qualifying can complicate and delay sale.

E. Seller financing contingency. I do not finance the sale of a property, unless it is for a very small loan amount, well secured (referred to as "carrying-back paper") and for a good reason. For example, a buyer wanted a building I was selling, but wanted a contingency to first sell a piece of land he had purchased with the intention of constructing a building on it, but later decided to purchase my building. He had financed the purchase of the land and did not want to have both that loan payment and a loan payment on the purchase of my building at the same time. I asked him how long he thought it would take to sell the land. He estimated six months. So, I offered to carry back a second trust deed loan for one year in the amount equal to one year of his loan payments for the land. And I said he could pay off my loan when he sold the land, which should easily be within the year. That satisfied his cash-flow concerns, so he bought the building. I carried-back paper in that sale because I had good security and it allowed the sale to proceed.

49. The Sale Agreement

Again, considering the cost of having an attorney draft a custom document, I prefer using a standard form obtainable from commercial real estate brokerage associations. They are easy to use, with fill-in-the-blanks, are replete with optional terms, and most also serve as escrow instructions. Any sale terms or contingencies that are not covered in the standard form can be attached in addendum form.

The following are examples of advisements, clarifications, disclosures, and disclaimers I attach as an addendum page to minimize the possibility of being sued later for some oversight. The language in such clauses should be structured to suit the particulars of your situation:

A. **Description of Property**. In Paragraph (number?) and on the Property Information Sheet the property is generally described as an approximately (number?) square feet industrial building on approximately (number?) square feet of land. The buyer herein acknowledges its understanding that said description is approximate only and that the buyer should perform its own measurements to confirm the property size, and that the purchase price is not dependent upon the property's exact size or subject to adjustment if the exact size varies from the aforementioned approximate measurements.

B. **Hazardous Substances**. Though previous tenants in the property might have stored or used minor quantities of household cleaners, pest control poisons, or petrochemical lubricants incidental to the maintenance of the property and operation of their businesses, the seller does not know of or suspect any hazardous substance contamination of the property. The buyer should be aware that some construction materials in older properties might contain asbestos, which is now classified as a Hazardous Substance. However, the seller has no actual knowledge of whether asbestos exists in any part of the property, nor any compelling reason to suspect it does.

C. **Disclosure** (if applicable). The seller, (name?), is a licensed (State name) Real Estate Broker with expert knowledge in industrial real estate. The seller is not acting in a brokerage capacity in this transaction; he is not representing either party and owes no fiduciary duty to the buyer.

D. **Advisement**. To ensure that the buyer's post-purchase expectations will be fulfilled, it is in the buyer's best interest to seek the counsel of qualified professionals to advise in purchasing the property. In particular, an experienced industrial real estate appraiser should provide the buyer with an opinion of the property's value to ensure the buyer is paying a fair price; and a certified public accountant (CPA) should advise on the taxation considerations; and an attorney should advise on the legal sufficiency of this and all related documentation including the escrow documents and all other relevant legal considerations. (NOTE: I suggest making this advisement if you are a licensed real estate agent or broker, to avoid a buyer or seller later claiming that they were taken advantage of in the transaction due to your superior business knowledge.)

E. **Disclaimer**. The seller makes no warranties as to the condition of the property, and advises the buyer that the property is being sold "as is." Consequently, the buyer should not purchase the property until the buyer and the buyer's expert advisors conduct appropriate inspections to determine if there are any defects or conditions that may cause the buyer to suffer adverse economic consequences.

50. The Sale Escrow

The sale escrow process is basically the same as the purchase escrow explained in **Subject 10**, with the buyer/seller roles reversed. Once the sale agreement has been signed by you and the buyer, the next step is to contact a reputable title and escrow company, such as First American or Chicago Title, ask to speak with an experienced escrow officer, and set an appointment to open escrow, at which time you will provide her with an executed copy of the sale agreement and contact information for you and the buyer. At this time, the buyer should make a "good-faith deposit" in an amount adequate to assure you that he is serious about the purchase, and which he will forfeit to you as liquidated damages if he fails to perform in the purchase without reasonable cause.

Because most formal purchase agreements also include the escrow instructions, the escrow officer need only prepare supplemental instructions that cite the sale agreement and deal with the escrow and title company's fees and conditions of service, a copy of which will be sent to you and the seller for endorsement. Make sure that the instructions have a paragraph stating that all documents can be signed in counterpart, so that you and the seller need not sign the same physical document.

The escrow fee is usually shared equally by the buyer and the seller. Incidental fees and taxes are borne by the buyer or the seller, depending on the custom in the geographic area in which the property is located, on which the escrow officer should advise you.

It is important to create a personal calendar of activities that are to be performed by you, the buyer, the escrow officer, and others, such as brokers, lenders, appraisers, inspectors, lawyers, tenants, and so on. The success of the sale (or any business transaction) is directly dependent on your attention to detail, timeliness, and management skills—you must manage the sale. It is imperative that you ride herd on everyone. The sale agreement and escrow instructions will delineate actions that need to take place by certain dates, and that, if not performed, will result in the termination of the sale and escrow. Two or three days before an action is required, I send an email to the obligated individual or parties reminding them of what is required, and confirm with the escrow officer that the act has been performed. If not, it might be necessary to draft an amendment to escrow granting more time to perform a particular act, to keep the sale agreement from failing. I do not solely rely on the escrow officer or involved attorneys to draft and send such reminders or to draft extension amendments; remember, if the purchase fails, the attorneys and escrow officer are still going to get paid. I usually draft such amendments myself, referencing the date, escrow number, property address, and the names of the seller and buyer, and state that this document hereby amends the subject escrow paragraph in the following particulars, indicating the new number of days or date change in the performance period. Then I print, sign, and scan it, and attach it to an email to the buyer with a cover note requesting that he sign it and deliver it to escrow. I later follow up with the escrow officer to make sure she received the amendment.

Contingencies typically have a time frame within which the buyer has the opportunity to state in writing his disapproval, in which instance the seller can cure the disapproved item or the escrow and sale will be terminated. If the buyer does not indicate a disapproval within the agreed time frame, the contingency shall be deemed waived and the escrow can proceed to funding and closing.

51. Business Relationships

As an industrial real estate investor, you are necessarily going to interact with a range of industry-related professionals. To optimize your investor experience, it is important that you develop rapport and, ideally, symbiotic relationships. To that end, I treat such professionals with courtesy and try to be helpful.

A. Appraisers. Appraisers are very important because they can stand between you either getting or not getting a loan to purchase a property; likewise, they can stand between a buyer getting or not getting a loan to purchase a property you are trying to sell.

If there is a financing contingency in your escrow, a property appraisal will be necessary. Appraisals can take from weeks to months to complete. The longer it takes to do the appraisal, the longer it takes to close an escrow; and the longer it takes to close the escrow, the higher the probability something will come along to negatively impact the deal. So, it is important to do everything you can to help the appraiser, which includes making the property available for inspection.

The appraisal must result in a valuation that supports the loan amount you or your buyer are seeking. So, it is important to provide the appraiser with value-adding information about the property, such as extra land, location attributes, and any special amenities. Also, try to provide comparable sales information that will support your desired value result. And, if you anticipate the appraiser might use some known comparable sales that do not support your desired value, try to point out any comparatively negative features of those properties that warrant their lesser values.

An appraiser is more likely to move quickly and render a valuation in your favor if he likes you. So, it is important to treat the appraiser with courtesy and respect, while at the same time not giving the impression that you are trying to pressure or control him or influence his results.

As an industrial building owner, you will occasionally be contacted by appraisers seeking lease rate or sale price information for the appraisal of a local area property they are doing. I provide them with such information and I ask them to provide me with a copy of their survey results for lease rates or sales values, which helps me stay abreast of the marketplace, so I can set appropriate lease rates for my properties.

B. **Attorneys**. Considering that most attorneys charge from $250 to $1,000 an hour, I use existing forms and rely on my own legal knowledge and negotiating skills whenever possible.

When selecting an attorney, I do a thorough due diligence investigation of his credentials and experience regarding the area of expertise I am seeking. I want seasoned representation and I definitely do not want to pay for an attorney to spend time educating himself on my subject area of law interest.

Most attorneys are ethical, but it must be considered that they are paid by the hour and you must pay them whether the purchase, lease, or sale transaction succeeds or fails. In transactions where both parties are represented by attorneys they tend to take over the transaction, pushing the principals and brokers to the side. Often, they get bogged down in arguing over minutiae, running up the bill, losing sight of the overall goal, and delaying the close—which invites failure of the deal. So, it is important that you maintain control of the attorneys, rather than let them control you.

If you are represented by an experienced commercial real estate broker, he should have expert negotiating skills and specific knowledge about the market and physical and financial aspects of the property you are considering buying, selling, or leasing. So, do not allow your attorney to interfere with your broker's representation or cut him out of the loop, regarding negotiating deal points or critical document wording. And never permit an attorney to suggest cutting a real estate broker's commission after you have entered into a representation agreement with the broker.

Though attorneys are trained in the law, that does not necessarily make them good negotiators or good businesspeople. I rely on attorneys for litigation representation and advice on the legal enforceability of contract wording and liability issues, but I am very careful about accepting their opinions on general business matters.

C. **Accountants**. A good knowledge of accounting is necessary to evaluate the financial statements and income tax returns of prospective tenants. If you do not possess such knowledge, you will need a certified public accountant (CPA) to assist you in qualifying tenants, and to advise you on real-estate-related taxation matters.

D. **Commercial Real Estate Brokers**. Commercial real estate brokers, and agents under their supervision, represent buyers, sellers, lessors, and lessees in real estate transactions. They can estimate (not appraise) the value of properties, market them, coordinate escrows, arrange financing, negotiate transaction terms, qualify tenants, and manage properties. They also draft purchase and sale agreements, leases, addendums and related documents, and advise on real-estate-related legal and taxation matters.

Whether or not you employ brokers to represent you, it is important to cultivate a good relationship with your local brokerage community, for two reasons: first, because you will need to rely on them to bring you purchase opportunities and prospective tenants; and, second, because they are a good source of the market information you will need to set proper lease rates for your properties.

(1) Finding a good commercial real estate broker

Drive around the area in which you wish to purchase or lease out an industrial property and note the names of the agents on the available property signs; or call a major commercial real estate brokerage company in that area, speak with the sales manager, and ask him for the name of the top industrial agents in the office. Then contact the candidate agents, set appointments to interview, and judge them on the following criteria:

a. Does he have at least five years' experience in industrial real estate in the geographic area in which you wish to purchase?
b. Does he practice attention to detail and timeliness?
c. Is he well-groomed and businesslike in appearance?
d. Does he have good client references?
e. Does he have a "broker" license (which requires more experience, education, and higher-level testing than an agent license)?
f. Does he hold a bachelor's degree or higher, preferably in business administration, with a specialization in real estate, economics, accounting, finance, or marketing?

Do not hire an agent simply because he was recommended by a friend, relative, or other acquaintance, unless he meets the above qualifications and is employed by a major brokerage firm or has his own well-established, independent industrial real estate brokerage office.

A professional broker will not represent a client unless it is under an exclusive representation or listing agreement, so be prepared to sign one. When I hire a broker, I limit the agreement term to no more than

90 days, which gives me adequate time to judge his performance; the agreement can always be extended if he is doing the job. Most exclusive representation or listing agreements have a clause that allows the broker, before the expiration of the agreement, to provide you with a list of the properties he has presented to you or the prospective tenants to whom he has shown your property. Those agreements guarantee the broker a commission if, within one year, you purchase any of the properties or sign a lease with any of the prospective tenants listed. I limit the number of such properties to no more than five buildings or prospective tenants, and limit the protection period to no more than six months. Having too many protected properties or prospective tenants will make it difficult to hire an alternative broker if you are not comfortable with the first one, because they would unreasonably restrict the alternative broker's representation.

E. **Commercial Real Estate Developers**. Commercial real estate developers plan, create, and oversee land sale subdivisions, industrial parks, and build-to-suit projects. They are a good source for purchasing new buildings that have standardized, marketable floor plans and amenities in well-planned commercial environments.

Developers can be very helpful in advising you on whom to hire to do roof repairs, HVAC work, asphalt resealing, cement work, landscape maintenance, and legal defense; they can also provide general advice on solving property and tenant-related problems.

F. **Property Managers**. Compared to other types of real estate investment properties, industrial buildings are relatively easy to manage, particularly considering that NNN leases require tenants to maintain the property in virtually all respects and to pay the property tax and insurance; and that gross leases require tenants to maintain the property, with the landlord having to pay only the property tax and insurance. Still, some investors might prefer to employ a property manager, particularly if the property is not conveniently located for the investor to manage it. If so, the typical fee runs between 2% and 10% of the gross rents collected, or a flat monthly fee—dependent on the work involved.

G. **Escrow Officers**. Having a good relationship with a competent escrow officer is a necessity, because they can move you smoothly through the property purchase or sale process, which can be particularly complex when multi-property exchanges are involved. Once you have found a good one, it is in your best interest to make sure they get a Christmas card every year.

H. **Insurance Brokers**. Commercial real estate property and liability insurance companies are typically represented by insurance brokers who act as wholesalers to agencies that retail the insurance to property owners. This presents a problem if you have an issue with your coverage wording or claims, because you have two levels of intermediaries between you and the insurance company—actually three, if it involves a claim, because insurance companies have claims adjusters with whom you must deal.

In my experience, the retail insurance agents are not particularly well versed in the details of policy coverage and they are reluctant to go to war for you in arguing with an insurance company. And, if you go around your local agent to the brokerage company representing the insurer, you are faced with the problem that they are "representing the insurer," not you. In some instances, I have gone directly to the upper management of national insurance companies to get problems resolved. It can be done.

I. **Tax Advisors**. When it comes to 1031 tax-deferred exchanges, your real estate agent, escrow officer, and exchange accommodator should be able to advise on and process such sale/purchase transactions. However, unless you have a good knowledge of the IRS Code, you will need an experienced tax advisor to assist you in filing your federal return for the year in which the exchange took place. For the "do it yourself" investor, I recommend purchasing the Federal Tax Handbook (published annually), which lists the Internal Revenue Codes and Regulations. This is an excellent source for guidance on commercial real estate matters, such as calculating capital gains, depreciation schedules, expenses versus capital improvements; and for defending yourself in audits.

52. Understanding Accounting — Everything You Need to Know in a Nutshell

After business school, I was employed for five years by the National Cash Register Company (NCR), marketing their accounting application computer systems. In that capacity, I developed accounting expertise that has benefited me in representing clients and in my own industrial real estate investments. One of the most important tasks in successful industrial real estate investment is performing effective due diligence investigations of prospective tenants, which I refer to as "the financial colonoscopy." To do so, it is necessary to review their financial statements and income tax filings, which requires accounting expertise. Because many investors do not have such expertise, the following is a condensed course in "understanding accounting," followed by a presentation on evaluating the financial statements of prospective tenants.

Accounting. The "Dual Entry" accounting system used by most Western nations was conceived by the Italians about 700 years ago. A business's accounting records, though now computerized, are often referred to as its "books," because accounting was originally done with pen and ink.

General Ledger. The "General Ledger" is a master file that contains all of the business's "accounts."

There are six categories of accounts: **"Assets," "Liabilities," "Capital," "Income," "Expense,"** and **"Profit (or Losses)."** Each subaccount in a category is identified with a number.

Assets are usually numbered in the 100s, Liabilities in the 200s, Capital in the 300s, Income in the 400s, Expense in the 500s, and Profit in the 600s.

- Assets are things a business owns, such as vehicles, tools, inventory, supplies, cash, real estate, prepaid taxes; for example, account #101 might be for Cash.
- Liabilities are a business's financial obligations, such as accounts payable, taxes due, equipment, auto and real estate loans.
- Capital is a business's "Net Worth," which is the difference between its Assets and Liabilities. Accordingly, the simple formula for the general ledger is: assets minus liabilities = capital (net worth).
- Income is the monies a business takes in from selling its goods or services.
- Expenses are the expenditures made to produce the income, such as labor payroll, and for materials used to make the products sold.

Income Statement. The "Income Statement" report is an accounting of the income and expenses and resulting profit or loss for a specific accounting period, usually done monthly. The total expenses are subtracted from the total income and the result is either profit or loss. The simple formula for the Income Statement is: income minus expenses = profit (or loss).

The profit or loss is then posted as an addition to or subtraction from the capital account, which increases or reduces the net worth of the business, and resets the income, expense, and profit accounts to zero, so they are ready to record the next month's income and expenses. Because the income, expense, and profit accounts are closed out to zero every month, they are referred to as "operating accounts," as distinguished from the asset, liability, and capital accounts, which are of a permanent nature.

Balance Sheet. The "Balance Sheet" report is a summary statement of the general ledger accounts, in which the total of the liability account balances is subtracted from the total of the asset accounts, with the result indicating the total of the capital account, which is the business's net worth. The balance sheet's simple formula is: assets minus liabilities = capital.

Financial Statements. A business's Income Statement and Balance Sheet are referred to as its "Financial Statements."

General Journal. The "General Journal" is a file used to make and record all of the plus and minus accounting entries (also called "postings") into the general ledger accounts. It serves two purposes: first, to perform the physical posting to the account; and, second, to create an audit trail of all accounting entries to the general ledger accounts, so that balance errors can be tracked down and corrected. Though computer files are now used, the words "ledger" and "journal" are used because, before computers, account entries were made with pen and ink into a physical paper journal, and postings were made with pen and ink to paper account ledger sheets.

Accounting is a "dual entry" system, which means each account posting must be offset by a counter-entry. The left posting column is for posting "Debits" and the right column is for posting "Credits." Assets normally have a debit balance, so a debit posting to an asset account increases the balance of that account, and a credit posting decreases it. Liability accounts normally have a credit balance, so a credit posting to a liability account increases its balance, and a debit posting decreases it. Therefore, since assets minus liabilities equal capital, the capital account normally has a credit balance, because a healthy business should have more assets than liabilities.

Income accounts normally have a credit balance, so a credit posting to an income account increases its balance, and a debit posting decreases it. Expense accounts normally have a debit balance. So, a debit posting to an expense account increases its balance, and a credit posting decreases it. Therefore, since income minus expenses equals profit, the profit account should have a credit balance, because a healthy business should have more income than expenses. When an entry is made in the general journal, the date, account number, and a subject description of the entry are recorded and the amount is posted in either the debit or credit columns. Because accounting is a dual entry system, an offsetting entry must also be posted. For example, to record a $1,000 payment of rent in the general journal, the rent expense account number will be referenced and $1,000 will be posted in the debit column; and an offsetting entry will be made referencing the cash asset account number and posting $1,000 in the credit column; thereby increasing the rent expense account balance by $1,000 and decreasing the cash asset account balance by $1,000. At the end of each day, the sum of all the general journal debit postings should equal the credit postings. If not, an error has been made. Each posting amount must then be checked for its accuracy and to ensure that an appropriate offsetting posting was made. When the error is located, a correcting entry must be made. Likewise, each month a trial balance of the general ledger is performed. If there is a credit/debit imbalance, a review of that period's general journal entries must be made to locate and correct the error.

Here is a simple accounting example: You are going to start a lemonade sales business with $100 of your own money. The first two entries in your general journal will be a debit of $100 to the "Cash" asset account and an offsetting credit entry of $100 to the Capital account. So, considering the formula that assets minus liabilities equal capital, you are in balance, because the $100 debit balance in the Cash asset account equals the $100 credit in the capital account.

Next, you buy some lemons and sugar for $20 and post a general journal $20 debit entry to the "Inventory" asset account, and a $20 credit entry to the Cash asset account. You have increased one asset account (Inventory) by $20 and reduced another (Cash) by $20, leaving a Cash account balance of $80. As you can see, those two entries offset one another, so you are still in balance.

Next, you pay some kids $5 to make lemonade from your Inventory supplies. You then post a $5 credit to the Cash asset account (leaving a Cash balance of $75) and a $5 debit to the Labor expense account; again, those two entries offset one another. Now, you post a $20 credit to the Inventory asset account and a $20 debit to the Materials expense account. Again, you have made offsetting account entries that balance one another.

Next, you pay the kids $5 to stand on the corner and sell the lemonade. You then post another $5 credit to the Cash asset account (leaving a Cash balance of $70) and a $5 debit to the Labor expense account. You are still in balance, because those entries offset one another.

At the end of the month, the kids give you $40 that they made in sales. You then post a $40 debit to the Cash asset account (increasing the Cash balance to $110) and a $40 credit to the Sales income account, which offset one another.

Now it is time to do an income statement and balance the accounts at month-end. The income account has a $40 credit balance from the Sales posting; and the expense accounts have a $30 debit balance from the two $5 postings to the Labor expense account and $20 posting to the Materials expense account. Next, you post a $40 debit to the Sales income account and $40 credit to the Profit account, reducing the Sales account to zero and increasing the Profit account to $40, still in balance. Then you post a $10 credit to the Labor expense account and a $20 credit to the Materials expense account, and an offsetting $30 debit to the Profit account, which reduces the Labor and Materials accounts to zero balances and decreases the Profit account to a $10 balance, still in balance, and which is the profit from the month's sales.

Because it is month-end you need to close out and transfer this operating profit to the Capital account. To do that, you post a $10 debit to the Profit account, which reduces it to zero, and post an offsetting $10 credit to the Capital account, increasing it to $110.

Your general ledger Cash asset account now has $110 debit balance, and your Capital account has a $110 credit balance, reflecting the $10 increase in your Net Worth because of the Profits from Sales. And, as you can see, the credits and debits offset one another on both sides of the equal sign, indicating that you are in balance and accurate.

This is "basically" how all businesses, small and large, do their accounting. Understanding it helps you evaluate a prospective tenant's financial statements to determine the health of the business and if it will be able to reliably pay you rent.

53. Reviewing a Prospective Tenant's Financial Statements

When qualifying a prospective tenant, you need to review its "Financial Statements," which are comprised of its "Balance Sheet" and "Income Statement." Ideally, the financial statements should be in "audited" form, which means they have been reviewed by a certified public accountant (CPA) and attested as conforming with proper accounting standards. In reality the financial statements provided by most prospective tenants are from their in-house accounting records, which are not necessarily accurate.

The words Debit and Credit will not appear in the financial statements. The Asset, Liability, and Capital accounts will be listed in summary as line items on their Balance Sheet; and the Income, Expense, and Profit accounts will be listed in summary on their Income Statement.

In reviewing a prospective tenant's balance sheet, their assets should exceed their liabilities by a healthy margin, and those that can quickly be converted into cash ("current assets") should be adequate to pay their financial obligations that are due within one year ("current liabilities"). The "Quick Ratio" is an often used measure, in which the total of a company's current assets (e.g. cash and accounts receivables) is divided by their current liabilities. A ratio of 1:1 is a minimal indicator of financial health.

The Income Statement should indicate an annual net profit percentage in line with the averages for the type of business being evaluated. Such averages are available through IRS database sources, where they are organized by Standard Industrial Classification (SIC) codes. And the income should comfortably cover the increase in rent that will result from leasing your building.

If the company is a sole proprietorship and the owner is running the company, in addition to employee payroll expense, a realistic expense for officer (the owner's) salary should also be listed on the Income Statement. Otherwise, the indicated net profit is overstated by the amount the owner should be taking as a salary, which is often the case in small businesses.

To help confirm the accuracy of the prospective tenant's financial statements, I request their federal income tax filing for the corresponding period, which should reflect the same profit and net worth numbers. If tax returns indicate lower profits than the in-house records, it might be an indication that they are not reporting all income or inflating operating expenses. Do not be swayed by large sales, gross profit, or asset numbers. Large net profits and net worth are the true indicators of financial health.

BUSINESS
BOOKS

Business Books

Business Books publishes practical guides
and insightful non-fiction for beginners and professionals.
Covering aspects from management skills, leadership and
organizational change to positive work environments, career
coaching and self-care for managers, our books are a valuable
addition to those working in the world of business.

Tomorrow's Jobs Today
Rafael Moscatel and Abby Jane Moscatel
Discover leadership secrets and technology strategies being
pioneered by today's most innovative
business executives and renowned brands across the globe.
Paperback: 978-1-78904-561-1 ebook: 978-1-78904-562-8

Secrets to Successful Property Investment
Deb Durbin
Your complete guide to building a property portfolio.
Paperback: 978-1-78904-818-6 ebook: 978-1-78904-819-3

The Effective Presenter
Ryan Warriner
The playbook to professional presentation success!
Paperback: 978-1-78904-795-0 ebook: 978-1-78904-796-7

The Beginner's Guide to Managing
Mikil Taylor
A how-to guide for first-time managers adjusting to their new
leadership roles.
Paperback: 978-1-78904-583-3 ebook: 978-1-78904-584-0

Forward
Elizabeth Moran
A practical playbook for leaders to guide their teams through
their organization's next big change.
Paperback: 978-1-78279-289-5 ebook: 978-1-78279-291-8

Readers of ebooks can buy or view any of these bestsellers by clicking on the live link in the title. Most titles are published in paperback and as an ebook. Paperbacks are available in traditional bookshops. Both print and ebook formats are available online.

Find more titles and sign up to our readers' newsletter at www.collectiveinkbooks.com/non-fiction

Follow us on Facebook at www.facebook.com/CINonFiction